I0807386

I enjoy and especially love when an author has filtered primary sources and written well about his or her subject. Our gratitude goes to Richard Russell, who has ably and gracefully given us Robert Henry, an extraordinary man, pretty well unvarnished.
—*Wayne Caldwell, author of* Cataloochee *and* Requiem by Fire

Embarrassed, I reluctantly admit that even though I pride myself on a thirty-year addiction to western North Carolina history, I was not familiar with Robert Henry. Now that I've "met" him, my education is more complete. Thoroughly researched and well written, Mr. Russell records the incredible life story of a successful and colorful character in western North Carolina during the early to mid-1800s. Not only is the book a valuable contribution to the preservation of Western North Carolina history, but Robert Henry himself, I believe, would also be pleased.
—*Marci Spencer, author of* Clingmans Dome: Highest Mountain in the Great Smokies

Richard Russell has compiled an intriguing account of the western Carolinas' Henry family, sharing new insight concerning the Battle of Kings Mountain and perhaps the only published account on the Battle of Cowan's Ford. Hence forward, in passing "the old Henry place" in Henderson County's Crab Creek Valley, I shall carry with me newfound wisdom and a rejuvenated respect for its forebears.
—*Terry Ruscin, researcher/photographer and author of* Hidden History of Henderson County, North Carolina *and* Hendersonville and Flat Rock: An Intimate Tour

A fascinating, well-researched account of Robert Henry, his family and the early days of the Sulphur Springs. In addition, Russell was able to relate Henry's complex legal battles in an easily understandable form.
—*J.L. Mashburn, author of* Hominy Valley: The Golden Years, Hominy Valley: Revisited *and* Asheville and Buncombe County: Once Upon a Time

Robert Henry
A WESTERN CAROLINA PATRIOT

RICHARD RUSSELL

Foreword by Wayne Caldwell

THE History PRESS

Published by The History Press
Charleston, SC 29403
www.historypress.net

First published 2013

Manufactured in the United States

ISBN 978.1.62619.145.7

Library of Congress CIP data applied for.

Notice: The information in this book is true and complete to the best of our knowledge. It is offered without guarantee on the part of the author or The History Press. The author and The History Press disclaim all liability in connection with the use of this book.

Robert Henry in his ninety-fourth year. *From John Preston Arthur's* Western North Carolina: A History *(1914)*.

Contents

Foreword, by Wayne Caldwell	9
Acknowledgements	15
Introduction	17
1. Beginnings	19
2. Declaring Freedom	25
3. Kings Mountain	29
4. Cowan's Ford	41
5. New Frontiers	49
6. Running a Line	57
7. The Professional	67
8. Husband and Traveler	75
9. Sulphur Springs	87
10. Transitions	115
11. Trouble in Paradise	127
12. The Twilight Years	143
13. Aftermath	153
Epilogue	163
Notes	167
Bibliography	179
Index	187
About the Author	192

Foreword

Robert Henry: Patriarch Unvarnished

Someone said that these days, a historical novel takes place in any time prior to cell phones. I have also heard that anything before 1974 is considered "historical." This makes me smile, because on the one hand, I remember 1974 very well, and on the other, I realize I am an antique, an outmoded scribbler of historical novels.

Good historical fiction makes characters believable in a setting true to their times. This requires research, which I enjoy and especially love when an author has filtered primary sources and written well about his or her subject. That applies to this volume about Robert Henry.

When I found Richard Russell and Karen L. Clinard's *Fear in North Carolina: The Civil War Journals and Letters of the Henry Family* (2008)—mainly the diary of Cornelia Smith Henry, Robert Henry's daughter-in-law—I reveled in the details. Here's what they planted, here's what fabric cost, here's how cold it was, here's what she's reading. But her several references to "old Mister Henry," some in a rather catty tone, made me want to know more about this crusty old man. Who was he? Where did he come from? Why was he off in Clay County?

Richard Russell's new biography answers those questions, adds much to our knowledge of early times in western North Carolina and limns a character who, some might think, is more at home in fiction than history.

America has birthed many such men and women. Think of the stories clinging like cockleburs to such people as George Washington and Benjamin Franklin, or David Crockett and Daniel Boone. I have also noticed that prominent men and women of the late eighteenth and early nineteenth centuries in western North Carolina were terribly hardy, and some were both brilliant and, well, mean. Or perhaps they were merely tough? Shrewd? Certainly. Tight as tree bark. Stubborn as ill-tempered mules. You get the picture. These are people like Thomas Stradley, the first pastor of Mount Pleasant Baptist (now Asheville's First Baptist Church).[1] He is said to have left England in 1828 with "his wife, five children, and a cow." One wonders if he also had a sack of magic beans, for when he died in 1891, he owned well over two thousand acres. He may have been a man of God, but I would suggest he was also a tad, well, mean. One had to be to prosper in those days.

If a Baptist preacher's story flirts with folklore, what about a man like Robert Henry? The first of the Henry family to settle in Buncombe County, as a boy, he had seen the Mecklenburg Declaration of Independence signed and had been wounded at Kings Mountain. So he was a Revolutionary War hero. Later, he helped survey the boundary between North Carolina and the new state of Tennessee. So he was a tough woodsman and a self-sufficient outdoorsman, potentially subsisting on mule meat.[2] Still later, in Buncombe County, he became a lawyer, physician and teacher before he resorted to a new profession, that of hotelier. So he was a jack of all professional trades.

By the time Henry died in 1863 (he was in his mid-nineties), he had owned thousands of acres in North Carolina and Tennessee and had owned many people of color, one of whom, Julia, is buried by his side in Tusquittee. He was a man more successful than most in western North Carolina's early days, and one about whom stories were told, most of them for the truth. They include several versions of his predicting his own death. But Russell is careful to let the reader know what is documentable and what might be, as Huck Finn called them, "stretchers." Henry was a man of substance—who would give a blunt opinion and fight you over it. I quote from his will: "I bequeath him [Robert Marcellus Henry] nothing…[because] his manner of life is well known." This, mind you, was his namesake child!

Like many another soul, Robert Henry had a drinking problem, which led to his eventual separation and divorce from his wife of thirty years. And

---

1. Charles Deweese, *The Power of Freedom: First Baptist Church, Asheville, North Carolina, 1829–1997*. Nashville, TN: Providence House, 1997.

2. See Russell's quotation in Bedini, "Early American Surveyors," 58. This, of course, makes Henry a potential character in a southern novel. See also Jerry Leath Mills, "Equine Gothic: The Dead Mule as Generic Signifier in Southern Literature of the Twentieth Century" in *The Southern Literary Journal* (Fall 1996)—the gist of which is, if it ain't got a dead mule in it, it ain't southern.

litigious? Lord, he and his son-in-law, Reuben Deaver, were constantly before the courts over one business or another. Robert Henry was a difficult man—complicated, bright, shrewd, may we say mean? He was a man who shared DNA with Crockett and Boone, the characters of Twain and Faulkner and any number of genuine American heroes—a man, in short, worthy of a book.

Perhaps one day, Robert Henry will provide the frame upon which to hang another historical novel. Although, like many in western North Carolina, I claim distant kinship to him—my second cousin Elizabeth Henry Laisy is a direct descendant—I'll not write it, but I'll sure line up to buy it.

In the meantime, our gratitude goes to Richard Russell, who has ably and gracefully given us Robert Henry, an extraordinary man, pretty well unvarnished.

—WAYNE CALDWELL

Among the whispering pines
A lonely grave there be,
They whisper day and night,
"Honor to Bob Henry."

The silent peaks stand by,
Their vigil ever deep,
Until the day our illustrious dead
Shall be called from his long, long sleep.

—*R.E. Crawford*[1]

Acknowledgements

Many individuals and organizations are deserving of my appreciation for their help and valuable contributions in the completion of this book. Without their assistance, it would not have been possible.

I am especially indebted to Elizabeth Henry Laisy for access to family documents and photos, for kindly permitting me to rummage through and scan personal papers for hours at a time and for always enthusiastically supporting this project. Thank you!

The assistance provided by the staff of the North Carolina Collection at Pack Memorial Library in Asheville, notably from Ann Wright, Zoe Rhine and Lyme Kedic, has been indispensable. I have enjoyed working with them over the past few years. They are always very professional, accommodating and knowledgeable, and I am grateful for their help.

In addition, I thank the archivists at the North Carolina Department of Archives and History; Jack D. Wood at the Tennessee Room of the Jackson/Madison County Library in Jackson, Tennessee; Karen Loughmiller at the West Asheville Library; Jane Johnson at the Mecklenburg County Library, Charlotte, North Carolina; Friedrich Hamer at the South Caroliniana Library in Columbia, South Carolina; Diana Sanderson at the Asheville School Archives; the staff at the Old Buncombe County Genealogical Society, Asheville, North Carolina, including Charles Haller, Sandy Samz, Ruth Dilling and especially Nancy Manning for granting access to her Buncombe County court records file; and Chief Ranger Chris Revels and the staff at Kings Mountain National Military Park.

Several descendants of Robert Henry willingly shared their knowledge of Henry family history. They are Zera Mackey, Melissa Mathews, Arbutus Aiken Hughes, John and Lynda Hancock and Doris Noland Parton. Also, I thank Dee Finney for posting volumes of information online. Thanks to Don Taylor for providing Robert Henry's survey book, documents and photos and for care and maintenance of the old Sulphur Springs Cemetery.

I thank J.L. and Emma Mashburn for conveying much local history and for publishing their excellent books, as well as Vance Pollock, Brotherhug Barlow and Steve Rasmussen for their research and efforts to preserve the history of West Asheville and the Sulphur Springs.

I am forever appreciative to Wayne Caldwell for graciously agreeing to read my manuscript and writing the foreword, and to authors J.L. and Emma Mashburn, Terry Ruscin and Marci Spencer for their kind words.

Finally, and above all, I thank my wife, Debbie, for her endless patience during the long process of researching, writing and rewriting. Her support has been valued more than she will ever know.

Introduction

On the afternoon of October 7, 1780, British major Patrick Ferguson and his Loyalist militia of over one thousand men were camped along the high ridge of Kings Mountain near the border of North Carolina and South Carolina. The American Revolution had dragged on for four years, and Ferguson had been dispatched by Lord Cornwallis to crush local resistance and gain Loyalist support in the Carolinas. While in route to Charlotte, Ferguson decided to reverse course and take a defensive stand against pursuing Rebels.

Robert Henry, three months shy of fourteen, stood poised at the base of the mountain with a courageous group of Patriot friends and neighbors known as the "South Fork Boys." The boys had come from their homes on the South Fork of the Catawba River in North Carolina to join forces with more than nine hundred rugged fighters known as the "Overmountain Men." The mountain men had tracked Major Ferguson to the ridge top, and now their forces surrounded the mountain, ready to attack. The South Fork Boys launched an assault up the northeast side of the mountain, and within minutes, young Robert Henry lay on the mountainside with a Loyalist bayonet impaling his hand to his thigh.

The following February, recovered from his wounds at Kings Mountain, Robert stood as one of the picket guards at a location on the Catawba River known as Cowan's Ford. He observed British soldiers on horseback attempting to cross, many being carried away or drowned by the swift current. He fired until a number of them reached his chosen signal rock in the river and then ran up the bank and took refuge behind a tree. He continued to fire as long as he could. With the tree's bark being loosened by enemy bullets, Robert narrowly avoided injury and was able to make an escape.

The zeal to fight for liberty may have been ingrained in Robert at a very early age. In 1775, while accompanying his father to Charlotte, he observed concerned and outraged citizens meeting and deliberating the Mecklenburg Declaration of Independence.

These boyhood experiences were surely influential and instrumental in preparing Robert for a remarkable life that spanned nearly a century. After the close of the Revolution, Robert studied law, medicine and surveying. He became an accomplished and prominent trial and land lawyer, one of the first in western North Carolina. He was appointed an official surveyor of the boundary line between Tennessee and North Carolina. He was Buncombe County's first teacher, and he also practiced medicine for a time.

Using surveying experience, knowledge of the law and contacts with Revolutionary War veterans, Robert amassed vast land holdings in North Carolina and Tennessee. Discovering naturally occurring sulphur and mineral springs on his land, he established a resort hotel, attracting more summer visitors than the nearby town of Asheville.

He was a landlord, a plantation owner, a farmer and a slave owner. Robert Henry has been described as versatile, a hero as brave as a lion, a philosopher and naturalist, a historian and author, an inventor, a genius and a pioneer. He was said to have a phenomenal memory.

Conversely, he was noted as slovenly and a bumpkin, a fraud and an imposter, and he has been called a liar.[2] He was known to be "fond of the bitters" and smoking. His appearance was more of the criminal than the defender. An eccentric man, he shunned normal attire and preferred to dress in the style of the native peoples, wearing moccasins at home. At times, he neglected to wear stockings when attending court. It is said he preferred sleeping on the floor rather than in a feather bed. His chief method of travel for less than a day's journey was by foot, using a large walking stick nearly as tall as himself.

At age forty-seven, he married Dorcas Bell Love, the seventeen-year-old daughter of Robert Love, founder of Waynesville, North Carolina. Robert and Dorcas Bell lived in Buncombe County, North Carolina, approximately seven miles west of Asheville, where they raised a large family. After thirty years of marriage, the couple was legally separated and then divorced.

Robert Henry was a man of legend, mystery and myth. His life was one of great achievement and one of tragic personal failure, yet his part in history remains unknown to most. A letter referring to Robert in an 1859 issue of *Harper's Weekly* stated, "Let honor be given to whom honor is due." Perhaps this writing will aid in achieving that goal.

Chapter 1

Beginnings

I, Robert Henry, was born 9th January 1767 in Mecklenburg County, N. Carolina.

Thomas Henry, Robert's father, was born about 1719 in Northern Ireland. His father, William, had emigrated there from Scotland, and this is where Thomas spent his childhood. When a young man, he was a soldier in the British army, and after completing his service, he settled along the Mersey River near Liverpool.

Eventually, Thomas left his home in England for America, either to escape religious persecution or to continue in military service. In the mid-1700s, using his skill as a carpenter, he concealed himself in a wooden box and had himself placed aboard a ship docked in Liverpool, bound for America. Thomas was active as a member of the Virginia Recruits and fought as a Virginia soldier during the French and Indian War. In the summer of 1755, he was near the battle at Fort Duquesne, in which British general Edward Braddock was defeated.[3] After living several years in his new home, and during a migration from Virginia to the Carolinas, Thomas's son Robert was born in a rail pen in the middle of the wilderness.[4]

This account has been recorded and accepted as true for well over one hundred years. How much of it is fact, speculation, misinformation or fabrication may never be known. North Carolina deed and estate records do verify that Thomas was a carpenter and joiner by trade, but the authenticity of the concealment anecdote is questionable. Could Thomas have accomplished such a feat on his own? Would family members or friends have assisted in the scheme? Thomas is thought to have been married in Ulster,

Northern Ireland, before leaving and then arriving at a port in Pennsylvania in 1746.[5] If so, his wife must have accompanied him on the journey. Would she have been complicit?

In the mid- to late 1740s, several Scotch-Irish settlements had been established near a major ford of the Catawba River in southern North Carolina. It is believed that Thomas's original plan was to settle in South Carolina or Georgia. Prior to reaching their intended destination, the Henrys were sidetracked in the backwoods of the North Carolina piedmont by the birth of their second son, Robert. Because few taverns existed for travelers, Robert was born in a "hastily built rail pen" somewhere near the South Fork of the Catawba River.[6] Finding the surrounding lands and waters so agreeable, Thomas abandoned his previous plans and made the family's permanent home near a crossing of the Catawba River known as the Tuckasegee Ford.

Early eighteenth-century maps illustrate the ford, approximately eleven miles west of Charlotte, as the only Catawba crossing within the boundaries of present-day Mecklenburg County. The Tuckasegee Trail was a key westward route long used by Native Americans traveling from the Charlotte area to the Blue Ridge in western North Carolina. The eastern approach is now on the grounds of the U.S. National Whitewater Center.[7]

Was Robert born in a common rail pen, typically considered a crude structure functioning only to confine livestock, and with no protection from the elements? Such a birthplace seems unlikely at first thought; however, the term "rail pen" defined several building types in pioneer days, including a settler's first dwelling. This temporary home was a covered shelter, usually built with round logs, or "rails," consisting of a single, small room, or "pen." A more commonly used term was "log cabin." These pens, or cabins, might be used for a short period of time, perhaps a few months or even several years until a larger, more permanent home could be built.[8]

Early Rowan County deeds indicate that Thomas Henry was a resident, landowner and cabinetmaker in North Carolina as early as 1763. On January 25, 1764, he executed a lease and release purchase with Francis Beatty for land on the south side of the South Fork of the Catawba River. He had a land grant of 600 acres near the Cherokee Ford in South Carolina, dated April 1764,[9] and also received a land grant of 168 acres located on the east side of the South Fork of the Catawba, dated September 26, 1766.

Robert Henry states that he was born on January 9, 1767, in Mecklenburg County, North Carolina, contrary to the generally acknowledged birth year of 1765.[10] His date of birth has been stated by others as January 10, 1765;

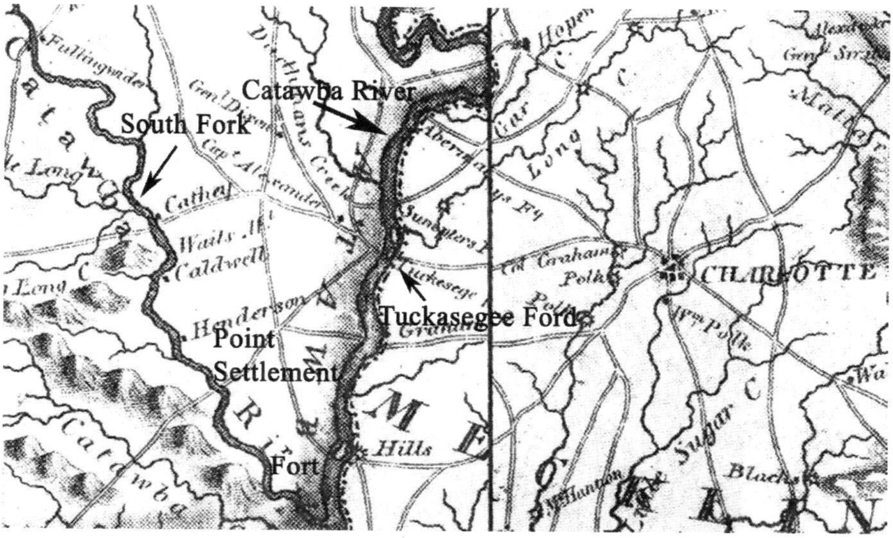

The Henry family owned and settled on land in North Carolina near the south fork of the Catawba River and the Tuckasegee Ford. Portion of an 1808 Price-Strother map with additional labeling inserted by author. *North Carolina Collection, Pack Memorial Public Library, Asheville, NC.*

February 10, 1765; and April 12, 1765.[11] If one references the early land deed records and accepts Robert's own stated date of birth or even the 1765 date, Thomas was already a resident and landowner in North Carolina years before Robert was born. It is doubtful then, that the Henrys' journey south had been delayed by the birth of Robert. They were already living there.

By 1765, the South Fork area had been settled for nearly twenty years by the Scotch-Irish. Henry families were living near the Catawba as early as 1748. William Henry, possibly a brother or relative of Thomas, enlisted that year for military service at an early defensive stockade and blockhouse, built where the Catawba and South Fork Rivers meet.[12] William later received a land grant and settled near the junction of the rivers in 1754. Sometime before or during the Revolution, William moved near Crowder's Creek onto lands he had purchased about 1768.

Another Henry family was living near the Tuckasegee Ford prior to 1753. This clan of Henrys, headed by another William Henry from Augusta County, Virginia, moved to the south side of the Catawba into present-day York County, South Carolina, in 1764.

Given that family history often has its basis in fact but over time becomes altered and/or misunderstood, there may be an alternative "birth in the wilderness" explanation. Thomas was likely intent on settling near Henry kin in North Carolina or possibly on his land grant in South Carolina. His first son, Joseph, was born on March 4, 1763, in North Carolina.[13] Is it possible that the delay of Thomas's journey was due to the birth of Joseph and not Robert?

Thomas Henry married a Welch woman named Isabella, born circa 1728, possibly the daughter of Robert Shields of Letterkenny, Ulster, Ireland.[14] When Thomas and Isabella married shortly before leaving for America, around 1746, Isabella would have been about eighteen. Thomas and Isabella were mentioned as husband and wife in a 1767 Mecklenburg County land deed.[15]

Jane Henry was born to Thomas and Isabella in 1762. Considering Thomas was forty-three and Isabella thirty-four at the time of Jane's birth, one would suppose previous marriages and/or children, but at present, no confirming evidence has been found. Additionally, Jane is noted as Thomas's eldest daughter in the will of his cousin Thomas Beattie (Beatty).[16] Henry men may have been inclined to marry later in life, as Robert Henry did not marry until age forty-seven, and Robert's son William did not marry until age thirty-three.

Thomas Henry died on September 27, 1787, at age sixty-eight.[17] Isabella died on December 30 or 31, 1821. Both are buried at Goshen Presbyterian Churchyard in Lincoln County, North Carolina. Thomas's estate was administered in 1790 by his son Joseph and another relative named Joseph Henry, probably a cousin. Records of an estate sale held in April 1791 name several family members as purchasers. Son Robert purchased a bay mare for twenty-one dollars.[18]

Historian F.A. Sondley states that Thomas and Isabella Henry raised a family of seventeen children, while another source states that it was Thomas's father, William, who had seventeen children.[19] In his personal notebook, Robert Henry directly or indirectly references only seven siblings. Henry family papers mention another, Thomas, who fought in the Revolutionary War and never returned. Known children of Thomas and Isabella are:[20]

Jane Henry

Jane was born about 1762, probably in Virginia, before the family migrated to North Carolina. However, Jane could have been born in North Carolina, as Thomas was a resident of Rowan County at least by January 1764. Jane died on April 20, 1837, and was buried in Smith's Cemetery in Belmont, North Carolina. She married Matthew Leeper (marriage bond dated March 18, 1782) in Lincoln County, North Carolina. Children of Jane Henry and Matthew Leeper were Matthew and James.

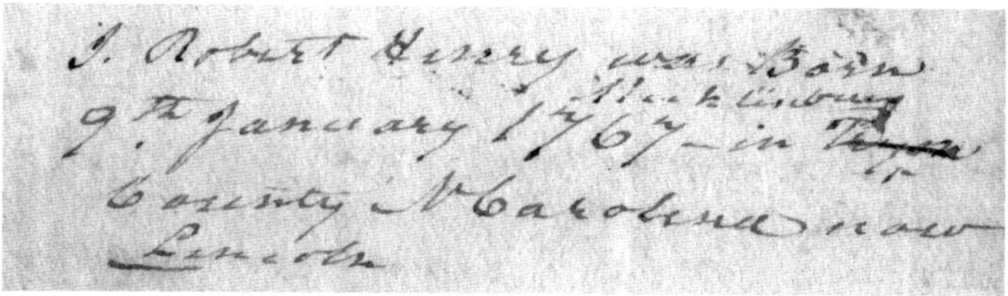
I. Robert Henry was Born 9th January 1767 — in Mecklenburg County N Carolina now Lincoln

Robert Henry recorded his date of birth in his personal notebook. *Henry Archive (private collection).*

Joseph Henry

Joseph was born on March 4, 1763, in North Carolina and died about 1840 at the age of seventy-seven in Henderson County, North Carolina. He was buried in Old Beulah Cemetery. Joseph married Elizabeth Porter on January 2, 1800, in Mecklenburg County. Children of Joseph Henry and Elizabeth Porter were Alexander P., Thomas, Ephraim, Margaret, Joseph, Albert, Noah and Robert. Joseph married his second wife, Charlotte Blythe, about 1820 in Henderson County. Their children were William Blythe and Rachel. There may have been a marriage previous to Elizabeth Porter.

Robert Marcellus Henry

Robert was born on January 9, 1767, in Mecklenburg County (now Gaston).[21] He died on February 6, 1863, in Clay County and is buried in Robert Henry Cemetery in Tusquittee.[22] Robert married Dorcas Bell Love, born February 9, 1797, on May 31, 1814. Children of Robert and Dorcas Bell were William Lewis, Mary Louise, Robert Marcellus, Elizabeth Isabella, Martha Ann and James Love.

Margaret Henry

Margaret was born about 1767 and died on September 14, 1835, at age sixty-eight. She married James Leeper (marriage bond dated March 4, 1795) in Lincoln County, North Carolina. James died on January 7, 1842. The couple had one child: Matthew Leeper of Arkansas.

Isaac Henry

Isaac was born on October 14, 1771, and died on May 17, 1861. He is buried in Goshen Presbyterian Churchyard in Lincoln County, North Carolina. Isaac married Catherine Barnett on May 30, 1800, in Mecklenburg County.

Children of Isaac Henry and Catharine Barnett were Nancy M., Thomas, Isabella, Dicy and Mary J. Isaac married his second wife, Mary Wells, on October 23, 1830, in Lincoln County.

Rachel Henry

Rachel, twin of John, was born on March 10, 1774, and died on September 18, 1838. She is buried in Goshen Presbyterian Churchyard in Lincoln County, North Carolina. Rachel married John McClure on December 20, 1792. Children of Rachel Henry and John McClure were Jane, Narcissa, Ezekiel and William.

John Henry

John, twin of Rachel, was born on March 10, 1774, and died without issue in July 1837. He is buried in Goshen Presbyterian Churchyard in Lincoln County, North Carolina. John Henry made his home at the family place.

Chapter 2

Declaring Freedom

The people threw up their hats and shouted.

In response to the Boston Tea Party in Massachusetts, the British Parliament passed a series of acts that American colonists believed were threats to their liberty. An important meeting was scheduled for May 19, 1775, at the Mecklenburg County courtroom in Charlotte for local citizens to discuss their concerns and disputes.

Thomas Henry, well established as a resident of the South Fork community prior to the onset of the Revolutionary War, had planned to attend, but there was a potential family crisis. Many foxes and dogs in North Carolina were infected with rabies and were becoming the source of a major outbreak.[23] Both wild and domesticated animals had become a serious health hazard, and Thomas's son Robert had recently been bitten by a rabid fox. Thomas feared for his son's safety, as well as that of his family, should Robert exhibit disease symptoms, so he took Robert with him.

Leaving home on Thursday, May 18, Thomas and Robert headed east toward Charlotte. Robert was riding his horse, the "Black Filly," and Thomas was walking. They may have traveled in or with a small wagon.[24] The first night was spent at Mr. McCreary's, just beyond the Tuckasegee Ford, and on the nineteenth, the pair traveled the remaining twelve miles. They witnessed a stir of activity when they arrived as "the people were gathering in from all the surrounding country." Attendees "commenced their deliberations in the court house that evening. He [Robert] recollects well McKnitt Alexander and Mr. Polk as active participants in the meeting."[25]

The Old Mecklenburg Courthouse in Charlotte, North Carolina, where declarations of freedom were made in 1775. *From* General Joseph Graham and his Papers on North Carolina Revolutionary History (1904) *by William A. Graham.*

While engaged in their discussions, the delegates received word that one month prior, the Battle of Lexington had been fought in Massachusetts. The delegates were outraged and, according to Alexander, passed a series of resolutions at about two o'clock that night. The May 20, 1775 resolutions became known as the "Mecklenburg Declaration of Independence." While the meeting continued late into the night, Robert lay sleeping behind the courthouse door on his father's "great coat." He awakened when hearing loud shouts of "declaring for liberty" and "passing the resolutions of freedom" and statements that this "would bring on war."

The signers proclaimed that the British government had "wantonly trampled on our rights and liberties and inhumanly shed the innocent blood of American patriots at Lexington" and that they did "dissolve the political bands which have connected us to the Mother country." They were now "a free and independent people."

Although he actively participated in the discussions, Thomas was ineligible to sign the resolutions. His home was in a section of Mecklenburg County recently formed into Tryon County and was therefore not a resident. While Colonel Polk was being qualified, he and Robert listened:

Robert Henry watches as delegates deliberate resolutions of independence. *Asheville Citizen*, March 1928. *Henry Archive (private collection).*

> *His father and he were present the next morning when oaths were administered to the parties present, either as committee men or as pledges to each other...he knew nothing of a legal or judicial oath; and when the oaths were being administered he listened attentively, but could not understand the import of the ceremony, and went to his father, who was in another part of the room, to inquire what they were doing, and his father replied that they were "swearing"; and he told him, "No, for he had listened to them, and they did not say any bad words." His father then explained what the nature of the oath was.*[26]

When the historic meetings ended, Thomas paid his tavern bill with sixteen coppers, and the pair began their return trip home. Predating the Declaration of Independence by over one year, the validity of the Mecklenburg Declaration is still debated today, but throughout his life, Robert "never had any doubt of what he had seen with his own eyes and heard with his own ears" and had "no patience with those who doubted the truth of the declaration." He was known to vouch his character on its authenticity.[27] A.T. Davidson stated:

> *He had a grand history in our struggle for independence, was at Charlotte when the Declaration of Independence was made, but, being a boy at this time, he did not understand the character of the resolutions; but said he heard the crowd shout and declare themselves freed from the British government.*[28]

Chapter 3

Kings Mountain

The flag was up—the Whigs then shouted Hurrah for Liberty!

Tryon County residents shared the anger of their Mecklenburg neighbors. The actions of the British army at Lexington and Concord were unacceptable. Accordingly, on August 14, 1775, they passed their own resolutions. The Tryon County Resolves declared it was all citizens' duty to take up arms and defend against "ministerial vengeance and despotism" and to "resist force by force in defence of our natural freedom & constitutional rights against all invasions." The local militia would be active until "a reconciliation shall take place between Great Britain and America."[29] All county residents were expected to sign the document. Curiously, although ardent Patriots, no Henry family signatures appear on the resolves. A number of the signers became pro-independence Patriots, known as Whigs, while others became Loyalists, resentful of being excluded from governmental matters by these Rebels.

Following the Declaration of Independence in Philadelphia, Tryon County Whigs knew their grievances would be solved only by war. Robert Henry saw his father supporting the cause for independence by serving as a private in the North Carolina Line. Thomas also furnished sundries and provided wagon hire to the North Carolina, Virginia and South Carolina militia. It wasn't the first time he had taken up arms to protect his family and defend threats to freedom in Carolina. In March 1771, Thomas Henry (Hendry) participated in a Tryon County expedition to fight the Cherokee.[30]

Fours years after the Tryon Resolves had passed, the Revolutionary War in the Carolinas was escalating. In 1780, the British army, led by Major General Cornwallis, met Rebel fighters in a bloody encounter at Camden, South Carolina. Thomas Henry and his son Joseph, who had entered the service in June, were among those at the August 16 battle in which American general Horatio Gates and his army were soundly defeated. It didn't look good for the Americans. Cornwallis believed he now had control of South Carolina and set his sights on conquering North Carolina. Rebel traitors at Camden were ordered to be hanged, and anyone opposed to British rule would be imprisoned. Cornwallis made it known that these measures applied to everyone and urged North Carolina Loyalists, or Tories, to aid in the capture of Rebel suspects and seize their arms and ammunition.[31]

Returning home after the devastating Camden loss, Thomas found an increased local resistance to the rebellion. Loyalist neighbors considered him a traitor and one of their targets. William L. Henry, a grandson of Thomas and son of Robert, wrote:

> *Thomas…came home and stayed around home. Sometimes the Tories made it hot for him, and he had to hide out. One evening after sundown, he came near his house and sat on the fence, where the Tories shot at him across a small field that surrounded the home, missing him. He ran past a clump of chestnut sprouts and turned and jumped in on the stump and was hidden by the sprouts when they (his neighbors) the Tories came near him, and hunting him, but did not find him. Each of his neighbors saying where he had shot "The Old Bear" (Thomas Henry).*
>
> *Thomas Henry was a very stout man, often carrying several guns, and he heard his Tory (neighbors) while he was concealed on the stump where they were going. It soon being dark, he crossed some swamps and got ahead of them, and as they were coming through to where he was, he shot and killed one or two of them, and then got ahead of them at a crossroads and killed one or two. On the two firings on them, he killed three—two at one time, and one at the other. The writer saw Henry's Tree in 1837, a large oak near crossroads, and it was as well known as any other noted place in Lincoln County.*
>
> *He (Thomas Henry) then left home and crossed the South Fork (of Catawba) River, and Robert and Jane had to cross the river (about five miles) to carry his provisions, and as they returned one time, some Tory neighbors asked where Thomas Henry was. Jane told them where, and Robert said to Jane it is a lie, that he was not there. Robert went across*

> *the river and hooted like an owl and found his father and told him what Jane told.*[32]

His place of concealment now revealed and his safety compromised, Thomas left for South Carolina, where he "joined Howard and Morgan" and returned to the fight.[33]

In the fall of 1780, a militia regiment consisting of South Fork men and boys was formed in Lincoln County.[34] William Graham was designated colonel, Friedrich Hambright was named lieutenant colonel and William Chronicle, major. Robert Henry and several of his friends were among the volunteers. After years of observing his father and brother supporting the Patriot war effort, it was Robert's opportunity to fight. He wouldn't have to wait much longer.

Cornwallis's army had moved into North Carolina and was in occupation of Charlotte. British major Patrick Ferguson was dispatched to clean up western North Carolina and recruit Loyalist supporters, whom he promised to protect from the "backwater" types. Ferguson captured and freed two of these backwater Mountain Men, sending with them a message to Americans across the Blue Ridge: if they did not halt their opposition, he "would march his army over the mountains, hang their leaders, and lay waste their country with fire and sword."

Ferguson's threat provoked the men greatly. Hundreds of the "Overmountain Men" gathered at Sycamore Shoals, Tennessee, and marched south, bent on destroying Major Ferguson and his army of Loyalists. Along the route, they were joined by militias from Virginia, North Carolina and South Carolina. Major Ferguson received news that the Mountain Men were approaching and on the first day of October posted a proclamation throughout the countryside to rally support:

> *Gentlemen: Unless you wish to be eat up by an inundation of barbarians, who have begun by murdering an unarmed son before the aged father, and afterwards lopped off his arms, and who by their shocking cruelties and irregularities, give the best proof of their cowardice and want of discipline; I say, if you wish to be pinioned, robbed, and murdered, and see your wives and daughters, in four days, abused by the dregs of mankind—in short, if you wish or deserve to live, and bear the name of men, grasp your arms in a moment and run to camp.*
>
> *The Back Water men have crossed the mountains; McDowell, Hampton, Shelby and Cleveland are at their head, so that you know what you have to*

depend upon. If you choose to be pissed upon forever and ever by a set of mongrels, say so at once, and let your women turn their backs upon you, and look out for real men to protect them.[35]

The warning's derogatory and inflamed language further strengthened the patriots' determination. The Lincoln County militia, including Robert Henry, who was "riding a very fine horse," left home to join the pursuit of Ferguson. On October 4, at Probit's place on the Broad River in South Carolina, the unit met up with a moving mass of Mountain Men. There, "Major Billy Chronicle, with twenty men, joined the army; no halt called, still proceeding on."[36]

On the evening of October 6, they arrived at the Cowpens in South Carolina; however, Ferguson was not there. He was camped near the Cherokee Ford, which lay east on the Broad River. A forced march to find Ferguson's troops was decided upon, and over nine hundred of the most able men and horses were selected to take part in the hunt.

Robert was in a position to overhear the leaders' movement and strategy discussions. When objections to his presence were raised because of his youth and what he might hear, the South Fork group said his name was Robert Henry and that he was "as brave as a lion, and despite his age was fit and proper in every respect."[37] Colonel William Campbell remarked to Major William Chronicle, "The lad whom he had with him should not hear their enumeration." Chronicle replied, "He was a son of Old Rugged and Tough, that his cheek was too well hooped to leak."[38]

The Overmountain Men gathered at Sycamore Shoals, Tennessee, and were joined by the South Fork Boys in South Carolina. *Courtesy of the National Park Service.*

View of Kings Mountain. *From Draper's* Kings Mountain and Its Heroes *(1881)*.

After a series of scouting and spying expeditions undertaken by Enoch Gilmer, one of Major Chronicle's men, it was discovered that Ferguson was camped at a deer hunter's camp located on a ridge between two creek branches. The camp was familiar to Major Chronicle and Captain Mattocks and was known as Kings Mountain. Instead of continuing on to Charlotte, Major Ferguson had decided to reverse course and take a defensive stand against the pursuing Rebels on the mountain ridge.

Assignments were made to each officer and instructions given where they and their men would be positioned. They were to surround the mountain. Beginning that evening, they marched thirty-three miles over an eighteen-hour period toward their destination. On the afternoon of October 7, Kings Mountain was circled by nearly one thousand rough and angry Overmountain Men and Rebel militia.

Initially, the Lincoln County men were to be commanded by Colonel William Graham, but shortly before the battle, Graham requested a leave of absence, stating he had received word that his wife was dying of colic. Henry later stated that "Graham was known to be a coward."[39] Since William Chronicle best knew the ground, he was assigned the leadership duties, calling out, "Come on, my South Fork boys!"

Battle of Kings Mountain troop positions. The South Fork Boys fought their way up the northeast face of the hill. *From Draper's* Kings Mountain and Its Heroes *(1881)*.

Henry and the other South Fork Boys positioned themselves at the northeast base of the mountain to prepare for the assault, armed with tomahawks, knives and Kentucky long rifles. When the battle progressed to their section of the mountain, Robert wrote:

> *Enoch Gilmer called on Hugh Ewing, Adam Barry and myself to follow him close to the foot of the hill. We marched with a quick step, letting Major Chronicle advance about ten steps before us, but further from the hill than we were, until we met the wing from the other side of the hill. Then, Chronicle having a military hat, but had let it down to shelter the rain from him, and had it not set up, clapped his hand to it in front, and raised it up, and cried, "Face to the hill." The words were scarcely uttered when a ball struck him and he dropped; and in a second, after a ball struck William Robb, about six feet from Chronicle, he dropped.*[40]

The boys re-formed with Lieutenant Colonel Frederick Hambright as their leader and continued their ascent up the steep grade. Robert took a stand by a log lying across a hollow.

Stepping one step back, I was safe from the British fire. I there remained firing until the British charged bayonet. When they made the charge, they first fired their guns, at which fire it is supposed they killed Captain Mattocks and J. Boyd; wounded William Gilmer and John Chittim. The Fork boys fired and did considerable execution.

I was preparing to fire when one of the British advancing, I stepped [back] *and was in the act of cocking my gun, when his bayonet was running along the barrel of my gun and gave me a thrust through my hand and into my thigh; my antagonist and myself both fell.*

Tumbling over the log, Robert lay quiet, keeping "dark" while two or three Patriot charges and retreats passed over him.[41]

The Fork boys retreated and loaded their guns. I was then lying under the smoke, and it appeared that some of them were not more than gun's length in front of the bayonets, and the farthest could not have been more than twenty feet in front when they discharged their rifles. It was said that everyone dropped his man. The British then retreated in great haste and were pursued by the Fork boys.

William Caldwell saw my condition and pulled the bayonet out of my thigh, but it hung to my hand; he gave my hand a kick and went on. The thrust gave me much pain, but the pulling of it was much more severe. With my well hand, I picked up my gun, and found her discharged. I suppose that when the soldier made the thrust, I gripped the trigger and discharged her—the load must have passed through his bladder and cut a main artery of his back, as he bled profusely.

Freed from the bayonet, Robert received word that the Patriot's flag was up, as three cries of "Hurrah for Liberty" sounded down the mountain. Hearing Ferguson had been killed, young Robert had a desire to see for himself. He found him shot in the face and the breast—and he saw fellow fighter Samuel Talbot turn him over and take his pocket pistol.

Still in pain and now becoming drowsy, Robert could no longer hold onto his gun, so he dropped it and went down to a nearby stream. Here he saw what he considered a strange sight:

When I got near to the branch, [I] *met David Dickey and Colonel William Graham riding his large black horse, wielding his sword round his head, crying at the top of his voice, "Damn the Tories," and ascended the hill.*

The charge to kill Ferguson during the Battle of Kings Mountain. *From Draper's* Kings Mountain and Its Heroes *(1881)*.

> *Having seen him get leave of absence at the commencement of the battle to see his wife, I was filled with excitement and a conflict of passions and extreme pain; but this brought on another set of feelings, that may be understood, but I am not possessed of language to describe.*

Robert proceeded to drink from the branch and then bathed his hand and thigh with the cool water. He wondered about the condition of Major Chronicle and William Rabb. He found they were both dead. Some of the boys were hauling Captain Mattocks and John Boyd down the hill, and Samuel Martin was carrying William Gilmer, who had been wounded in the thigh.

> *Several of the South Fork boys were desirous to start for home that night, and were desirous to know how many were killed on each side. Joseph Beatty and Enoch Gilmer were appointed for that purpose of counting. They reported that 248 British and Tories were killed and that 143 Whigs were killed. They gave no account of the wounded. In the meantime, Hugh Ewing, Andrew Barry and Nathaniel Cook brought their horses and mine; put me on my horse, but could not take my gun. We rode over the battle-*

grounds; saw in some places the dead lay thick, and other places thin. We went about five miles from the battleground and staid [sic] *for the night. My wounds pained me extremely. Sunday morning we started for home. When we came to the South Fork, the waters were high, and my company would not suffer me to ride the river, but took me across in a canoe and hauled me home in a slide.*

According to Robert, "No Tories were hanged on the day of battle. They [the Whigs] lay on the ground Saturday night. On Monday, they hanged nine at Walker's."[42]

Robert arrived at home late in the day on Sunday. The bayonet had injured him badly. The first easing of his pain came when his mother made a poultice of wet ashes and applied it to his wounds. By sunrise the next morning, friends Hugh Ewing and Andrew Barry came to check on him. Soon, several men appeared at the door calling themselves Neutralists, whom Robert said were really Tories, to hear news about the battle. A conversation took place amongst them, Ewing and Barry:

Tory: Is it certain that Colonel Ferguson is killed and his army defeated and taken prisoners?

E and B: It is certain, for we saw Ferguson after he was dead, and his army prisoners.

Tory: How many men had Colonel Ferguson?

E and B: Nearly 1,200, but not quite 1,200.

Tory: Where did they get men enough to defeat him?

E and B: They had the South Carolina and Georgia Refugees, Colonel Graham's men, some from Virginia, some from the head of the Yadkin, some from the head of the Catawba, some from over the mountains, and some from everywhere else.

Tory: Tell us how it happened, and all about it.

E and B: We met at Gilbert Town and found that the foot troops could not overtake Ferguson, and we took between six and seven hundred horsemen, leaving as many or more footmen to follow; and we overtook Ferguson at Kings Mountain, where we surrounded and defeated him.

Tory: Ah! That won't do. Between six and seven hundred to surround nearly 1,200. It would take more than 2,000 to surround and take Col. Ferguson.

R and B: But we were all of us blue hen's chickens.[43]

Tory: There must have been of your foot and horse in all over 4,000. We see what you are about, that is to catch Lord Cornwallis napping.

The Tories departed, and it was reported that they immediately crossed the river and informed Cornwallis of the defeat. Cornwallis left Charlotte on October 12, 1780. Sometime after his retreat, Robert, his wounds still healing, had occasion to be in Charlotte. While there, he talked with David Knox, who told him he had been a prisoner in the street in Charlotte the Monday after the battle. He continued:

An officer came to the officer of the guard, and the following dialogue took place:

The first officer said to the officer of the guard, "Did you hear the news?"

Officer of Guard: No, what news?

First Officer: Col. Ferguson is killed, and his whole army defeated and taken prisoners.

Officer of Guard: How can that be? Where did the men come from to do that?
First Officer: Some of them were South Carolina and Georgia Refugees, some from Virginia, some from the head of the Yadkin, some from the head of Catawba. Some from over the mountains, and some from everywhere else. They met at Gilbert Town, about 2,000 desperadoes on horseback, calling themselves blue hen's chickens, started in pursuit of Ferguson, leaving as many footmen to follow. They overtook Colonel Ferguson at a place called Kings Mountain; there they killed Colonel Ferguson, and after surrounding his army, defeated them and took them prisoners.

Officer of Guard: Can this be true?

First Officer: As true as the gospel, and we may look out for breakers.

Officer of Guard: God bless us.

Whereupon David Knox jumped on a pile of fire-wood in the street, slapped his hands and thighs, and crowed like a cock, exclaiming, "Day is at hand!" Hence he was called Peter's Cock—having some analogy to the crowing of the cock when Peter denied his Lord the third time.

It was generally considered about Charlotte and elsewhere that this exaggerated account, given by the Neutralists, of Colonel Campbell's army, foot and horse, at 4,000, which carried a strong air of plausibility with it, was the reason why Lord Cornwallis immediately left Charlotte in the night, after the waters were passable, and did not stop day nor night until he met General Leslie at or near Winnsborough.

Chapter 4

Cowan's Ford

We pushed them into the water, they floated off, and went each to his own home.

By the end of January 1781, the course of the war was turning. Ferguson had been defeated at Kings Mountain, and Banastre Tarleton had suffered a disastrous loss in South Carolina. Morgan and his men, who had defeated Tarleton, were retreating northeastward across North Carolina with British prisoners and supplies taken during the Patriot victory at the Cowpens. Cornwallis was in pursuit and hoped to retrieve the prisoners and stop Morgan before he reached and crossed the Catawba River. Among Morgan's men was Thomas Henry, who had joined with Howard and Morgan after fleeing the Tory harassment and attempts on his life.

Thomas's son Joseph was serving a second tour as a private with Colonel Francis Locke, marching through Lincoln, Mecklenburg, Rowan and Guilford Counties.[44] Robert Henry was at home beginning studies under the tutorage of Robert Beatty, who was teaching at a small school near the Tuckasegee Ford. Classes were in session only three days when schoolmaster Beatty interrupted his class to make an announcement. He had received news that Cornwallis was camped at Forney's place about seven miles from the schoolhouse and that Tarleton was reported to be in the area looking for Whig boys, who when captured, would be forced to be musicians in the British army. School was quickly dismissed so that the students could go home and spread the alarming news.

That evening, Robert was joined by friends Moses and Alexander Starret, George and Robert Gillespie and Charles Rutledge, all of whom were fearful of being captured:

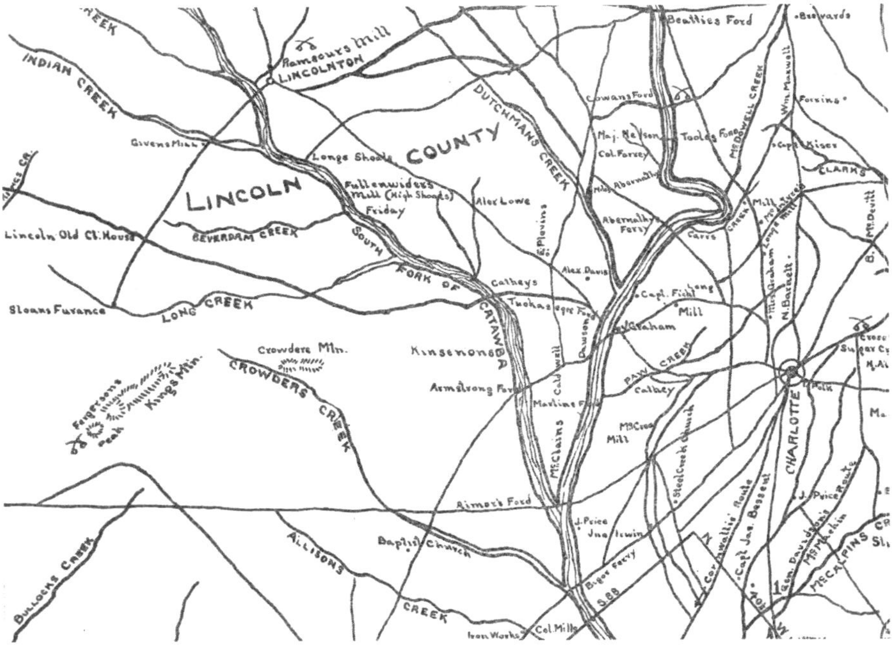

Portion of a 1789 map of Mecklenburg County depicting major waterways, fords, roads and battle sites, including Kings Mountain and Cowan's Ford. *From* General Joseph Graham and His Papers on North Carolina Revolutionary History *(1904).*

> *We lay out that night, and shortly before day-light, my brother, Joseph Henry, who had left the army to give the news, had crossed Catawba at John Beattie's in a canoe; and when he left the army, it was expected that Cornwallis would cross the river at Tuckaseage* [sic] *Ford.*[45]

That was all the boys needed to hear. Early the next morning, Robert, his companions and his brother Joseph crossed to the eastern bank of the Catawba at Beattie's, about two miles below Tuckasegee Ford, and then hid their canoe.[46] After spending some time at Beattie's, the group headed north to the Tuckasegee Ford, expecting it would be the location the British had chosen to attempt their crossing. Learning the enemy was instead near Cowan's Ford, the boys continued up the river, arriving at John Nighten's place about a mile and a half from the Ford.

Mr. Nighten gave them potatoes to roast and whiskey to drink. When they became "noisy and mischievous," Nighten cut off the whiskey, but by then, it had already helped to embolden the patriots. Robert daringly suggested that if someone would give him a gun and ammunition, they should go to the American army camp at Cowan's Ford. He was given a gun by his brother Joseph, and Charles Rutledge received one from Moses Starret.

Henry and Rutledge further equipped themselves by paying Nighten a $100 Continental bill for a pint of whiskey, which they promptly "dispatched." Joseph paid another $100 Continental bill for half a bushel of potatoes.

While Henry and Rutledge were making their way to the ford, Cornwallis was camped farther north near Beattie's Ford. He found that the river was so swollen from days of rain and the current so strong that it was impossible to cross. He had been delayed for two days. This gave the men under Morgan time to further their advance across North Carolina and the Americans time to place men on the eastern exits of the fords on the Catawba, their mission to slow the crossing and, therefore, the progress of Cornwallis.

When the waters began to subside, Cornwallis moved a small part of his army to Beattie's Ford to give the impression that the British army would cross there. But during the night, as the Americans were resting, Cornwallis moved the rest of his forces six miles south to Cowan's Ford.

General William Lee Davidson, a veteran of George Washington's Continental Army, was stationed with three hundred North Carolina militia four miles north of Cowan's at Beattie's Ford, where the decoy British army had been positioned on the opposite bank. General Davidson sent a company of cavalry under the direction of Joseph Graham and William Polk south to patrol Cowan's Ford and prevent a British crossing.

Cowan's Ford was actually two fords: a wagon ford going straight across the river, and a longer and more shallow horse ford that angled to the southeast about midstream. That evening, Davidson and another detachment went to the ford and set up camp on the Mecklenburg (eastern) side, about half a mile from the river at the horse-ford exit. This was where Cornwallis was expected to cross. Picket guards were posted near the wagon-ford exit.

Robert and Charles were welcomed by Davidson's guard of about thirty. They were told by an officer that Cornwallis was expected to attempt a crossing that night or in the morning and that they should choose their stands. Robert chose one close to the "getting out place," while Rutledge chose one on higher ground. Robert examined his stand and was "well pleased with it—for in shooting, if I would miss my first aim, my lead would range along the British army obliquely and still do damage, and that I could stand it until the British would come to a place the water was rippling over a rock, then it would be time to run away."

While Robert did not recognize any of the other men or boys except Joel Jetton, he did notice that Charles Rutledge had been joined on the higher

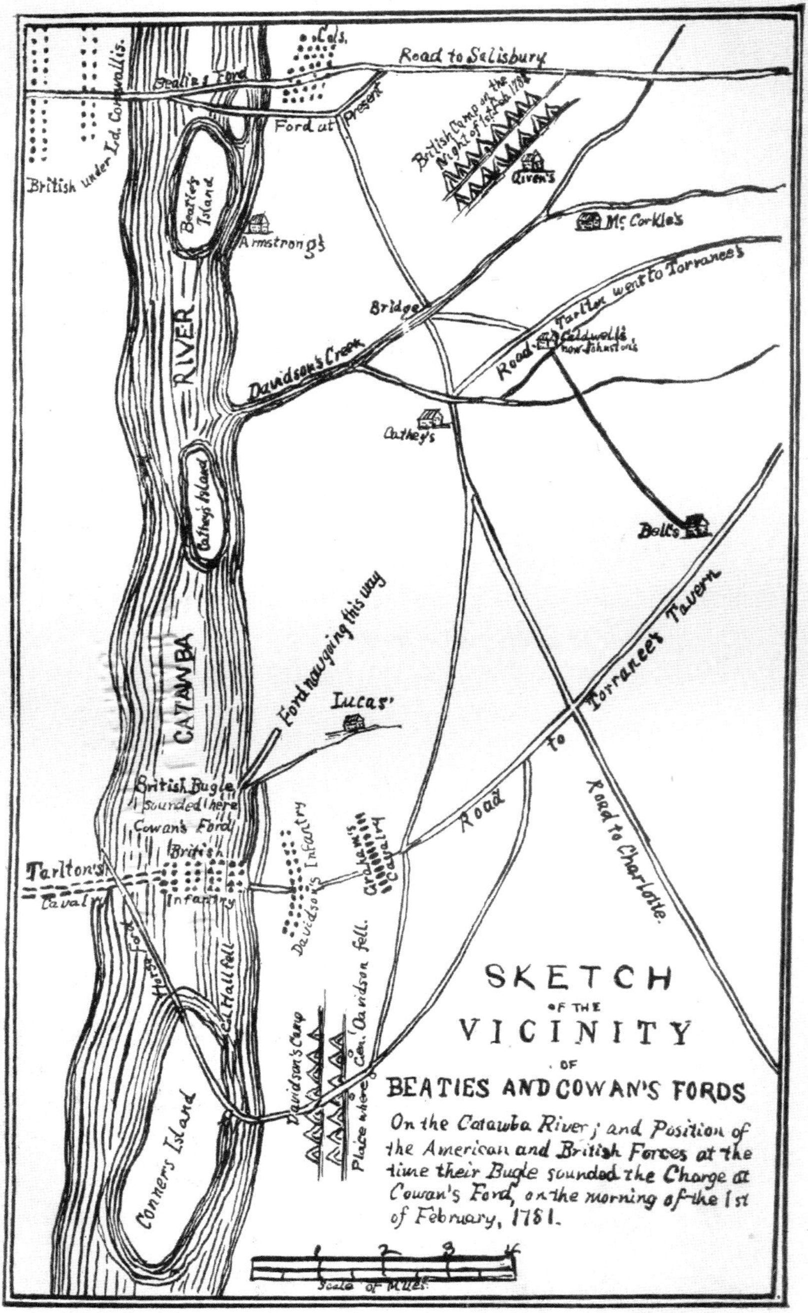

Robert Henry took a stand near the "getting out place" at Cowan's Ford. *From* General Joseph Graham and His Papers on North Carolina Revolutionary History *(1904)*.

ground by his schoolmaster, Robert Beatty. He was unaware that his father and brother were also in the area.[47]

The sound of an owl hooting was heard from across the river—a scout's signal that all was quiet at Cornwallis's camp—so the guard rested for the night. At daybreak on February 1, 1781, Joel Jetton awoke to the sound of horses struggling in the water. Finding the river sentry asleep, Jetton kicked him into the river and tried to fire his gun, which did not fire because it was wet. Running back to the camp, he yelled, "The British! The British!" Finding another gun, he fired, waking the rest of the guard.

Robert rushed to his position near the ford and upon seeing British red threw water in his disbelieving eyes thinking it must be from lack of sleep. But then he heard the rest of the guard firing and the sounds of splashing and drowning. The British had been led by their pilot into the deep "swimming water" (wagon ford) instead of the more shallow water used for horse crossing. To make matters worse, the river was still swollen from the recent rains; it was waist deep or deeper in some places, and the current was swift and strong. Robert fired until he saw British pilot Dick Beal preparing to shoot, and when Beal passed Robert's warning rock, Henry retreated up the riverbank.

From his camp nearby, General Davidson heard the firing and rushed to the scene, arriving just as the Americans were getting ready to retreat. As soon as he dismounted his horse, he was hit by a British rifle ball.

At the top of the riverbank was Robert Henry:

> *William Polk's horse breasted me, and General Davidson's horse, about twenty or thirty feet before Polk's horse, and near to the water's edge. That moment, Polk wheeled his horse and cried, "Fire away, boys; there is help at hand!" Turning my eye round, designing to run away, I saw my lame school-master, Beatty, loading his gun by a tree; I thought I could stand it as long as he could, and commenced loading. Beatty fired, then I fired, the heads and shoulders of the British being just above the bank; they made no return fire; silence still prevailed. I observed Beatty loading again; I ran down another load; when he fired, he cried, "It's time to run, Bob!" I looked past my tree and saw their guns lowered and then straightened myself behind my tree. They fired and knocked off some bark from my tree.*

A bullet struck Beatty, breaking the upper end of his thighbone, a wound that would later prove fatal. As he fell, he continued to yell for Robert to run. So Robert did. He ran as fast as he could for about one hundred yards, at which point his rational mind began to speak. The British probably did not have any horsemen that would follow, he thought, and the army would be at the riverbank for a battle. So he turned around and headed back to the ford, where he sat by a large tree, about fifty yards from the British. He exchanged fire with the enemy and found return fire came no closer to him than about thirty feet. Robert saw that "the whole of the Americans had left their stands or posts at the water's edge and judiciously fled, lest the British might hem them in by the river." Seeing no battle as he had anticipated, Robert soon retreated and decided to return back down the river to John Beattie's, where he and his friends had previously left their canoe. He wrote:

> *There I found my company, the two Starretts and two Gillespies, my brother Joseph and my comrade, Charles Rutledge. I returned the gun to my brother after counting the cartridges, found seven missing, therefore I had fired seven times, as I supposed.*

The next morning, the boys took their canoe and crossed back over the Catawba into Lincoln County. Neighbor James Cunningham operated a fish trap nearby, which they decided to check. The trap was cluttered with the bodies of fourteen dead men, several of whom they supposed had drowned, as they could see no wounds. "We pushed them into the water, they floated off, and went each to his own home." Neighbors reported even more dead at Thompson's fish dam and trap, tangled in brush and lying on the banks, and the "river stunk with dead carcasses."

The skirmish at Cowan's Ford slowed the crossing of British forces, allowing the Americans to retreat to the Guilford Courthouse near Greensboro, where General Greene and Lord Cornwallis would battle on March 15, 1781. Robert's father, Thomas, was with Greene's forces during the retreat from Cowan's Ford and when Greene moved to Wilmington and into South Carolina. There he participated in the Battle of Eutaw Springs. The men were "half-baked" and "lacking in food." Thomas came home broken down with rheumatism. Joseph Henry was in the retreat but had been discharged before the Guilford march.[48]

Years later, Robert penned his recollections of Cowan's Ford in response to what he considered errors in the 1851 book *Historical Sketches of North Carolina*, by Colonel John H. Wheeler. But Robert's view of events did not agree with those of Major William A. Graham, one of General Joseph Graham's descendants. In 1906, William Graham published his own version disputing some of Robert's observations, stating, "I deem it unnecessary to refer in this connection to the 'Henry Pamphlet' concerning this battle. Reference is made to it in Gen. Jos. Graham and his Revolutionary Papers. The questions in this paper from the British commanders corroborate General Graham's statements even more fully."[49]

However, Robert's version is considered a trustworthy account by a fighter present on the front lines, and a very detailed analysis was done by Chalmers Gaston Davidson in 1951 comparing the independent accounts of several participants, in which Davidson stated that Henry's memory was "nothing short of phenomenal."[50] In addition, Judge David Schenck stated:

> *Henry's account of the Battle of Cowan's Ford is totally different than that given by Gen. Graham, which latter I adopted in my history.*[51] *If I had seen Mr. Henry's account before I wrote my book, I certainly would have adopted it. It bears the impress of truth and is a narrative by one who was an actor in the scene and is entirely consistent with the whole surroundings. I feel sure that no true account of the Battle of Cowan's Ford has been published except this.*[52]

Chapter 5

New Frontiers

Indian, what did you die for?

Subsequent to Cornwallis's surrender and the conclusion of the Revolutionary War, Thomas, Robert and Joseph Henry returned to their homes and families along the Catawba River. Thomas was paid £60.15.8 for services in the North Carolina Line and received £9,540 for furnishing sundries and wagon hire to the militias of North Carolina, South Carolina and Virginia.[53] Thomas served as Lincoln County constable in Captain Moore's district for one year beginning April 1782. He probably stayed in Lincoln County until his death in 1787, at age sixty-eight. Robert and Joseph, however, were not content to remain near their boyhood home. Just as their father left his homeland many years before, they were compelled to move on.

Land west of the Blue Ridge Mountains was reserved for the Cherokee in 1763, but encroachment by white settlers did not stop. In an effort to rid their homelands and hunting grounds of intruders, the Cherokee aligned themselves with the British, both before and during the Revolutionary War. They executed raids on the illegals, killing dozens of homesteaders.

In September 1776, the North Carolina State Militia sent an expedition of over two thousand volunteers, including numerous Lincoln (then Tryon) County men, into Cherokee territory to put an end to the raids. Led by General Griffith Rutherford, the party assembled at Davidson's Fort (now Old Fort), marched west through the Swannanoa Gap and continued to the Cherokee villages. Many had already been abandoned, as the Cherokee were aware of the militia's movement. Nonetheless, Rutherford's men destroyed and burned everything along the path of the "Rutherford Trace."

The Cherokee were utterly defeated, their homes, crops and livestock all gone, and in July 1777, they ceded all lands east of the Blue Ridge Mountains. After the Treaty of Paris was signed in 1783, the United States claimed all Cherokee land east of the Mississippi River. North Carolina could now legally open all its mountain territory for settlement.

The beauty of the land across the Blue Ridge was etched in the memory of those who had participated in the Cherokee Expeditions:

> *Where the bottom lands were extensive as along the Swannanoa, lower Cane Creek, Mills River and especially along the upper French Broad, there were prairies, large for a mountain country and, wherever the terrain was low, rolling hills...the steeper and rougher hills supporting heavy stands of oak.*[54]

> *The land consists of vallies* [sic] *and mountains. The general growth of the timber is walnuts black and white, locusts, sugar trees, buck eyes, lyms, poplars & oaks of every description; the black & white hickory grows very plentiful—a great number of wild cherry & cucumber trees are to be found throughout our lands...buck eyes measuring thirteen feet round the body & black walnuts near the same size.*[55]

The state made land grants available to anyone who followed the filing procedure and could afford them. A written claim, along with a general description of the tract boundaries, was registered with the elected county entry taker. After the entry taker completed his paperwork and a waiting period of three months had passed, an order, or warrant, was issued to the county surveyor. He would then survey, prepare plats, give accurate boundary descriptions and indicate the number of acres.

The plats and survey warrant were sent to the office of the secretary of state, authenticated by the governor, signed by the secretary of state and recorded. The state became the grantor, and the claimant the grantee. The grantee then had twelve months to register the grant in the county where his land was located.

Enticed by land grants and perhaps a prematurely diminished fear of Cherokee raids, many men of the Revolution began filing claims and moving

Opposite, bottom: The Swannanoa River and Black Mountains, circa 1883–84. *North Carolina Collection, Pack Memorial Public Library, Asheville, NC.*

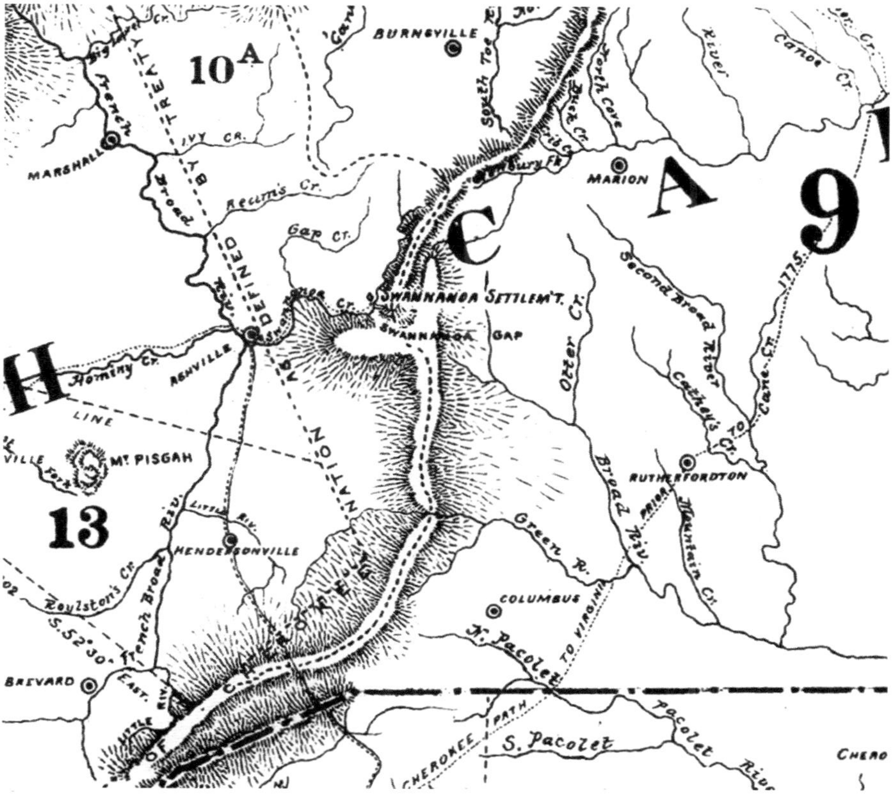

The Swannanoa Settlement was populated by Revolutionary War veterans a few years after the war. This map, drawn by C.C. Royce in 1884, shows the former territory of the Cherokee Nation of Indians. *North Carolina Collection, Pack Memorial Public Library, Asheville, NC.*

into an area now known as Buncombe County. Members of the Vance, Davidson, Alexander, Moore, Smith and Weaver families were among the first to settle, and shortly thereafter were joined by Joseph "Entry Taker Joe" Henry, a cousin of Robert Henry.[56]

Around 1784, Colonel Samuel Davidson constructed a log cabin in the valley of the Swannanoa River. He was soon lured away from his home, it is said, and scalped and killed by a band of Cherokees. In 1785, his twin brother, Major William Davidson, with his brother James Davidson and brothers-in-law John Alexander and Daniel Smith, established a settlement between Black Mountain and Asheville at the mouth of Bee Tree Creek, a tributary of the Swannanoa River. This became known as the "Swannanoa Settlement."

Colonel David Vance settled in the Reems Creek Valley. John Weaver settled in an area that is now Weaverville. Captain William Moore settled south and west in the vicinity of Hominy Creek. Robert Henry would someday be one of his neighbors. Captain Moore was familiar with the Hominy Creek area, where he had camped during his days on the Indian campaigns with General Griffith Rutherford.

The David Vance homestead on Reems Creek, near Weaverville in Buncombe County, was built by Vance after arriving from Burke County in 1788. *North Carolina Collection, Pack Memorial Public Library, Asheville, NC.*

Interesting folklore is associated with Moore's encampment. While he and his men camped within a horseshoe-shaped bend of Hominy Creek near the mouth of Caney Creek (or Branch), predatory wolves were carrying off their provisions. To remedy the situation, some manner of poison was left in or near one of the small branches of the creek. An Indian who had been secretly observing the movements of the soldiers became severely ill and subsequently died. Having quenched his thirst from the waters of Caney Creek, he surmised it had been the cause of his sickness and impending death. "The Indian's Curse" was placed on the vicinity of the stream, whoever had poisoned it and anyone associated with it.[57]

The unfortunate Cherokee was buried nearby, in a sitting position, on the northwest side of an ancient white oak known for many years as the Township Tree. One hundred years ago, evidence of the grave was still visible, rising about one foot in elevation. The giant oak still stands today on a knoll near Caney Creek.

Local children were often told to go to the tree, knock three times and ask, "Indian, what did you die for?" and that the answer would be, "Nothing at all." When they complied but heard no voice, the enticer would laugh and say, "I told you the answer would be nothing at all!" Sometimes, a trickster would hide behind the tree and provide the expected response.[58]

Colonel William Davidson soon settled on the east side of the Swannanoa and French Broad Rivers near present-day Biltmore Avenue in Asheville.

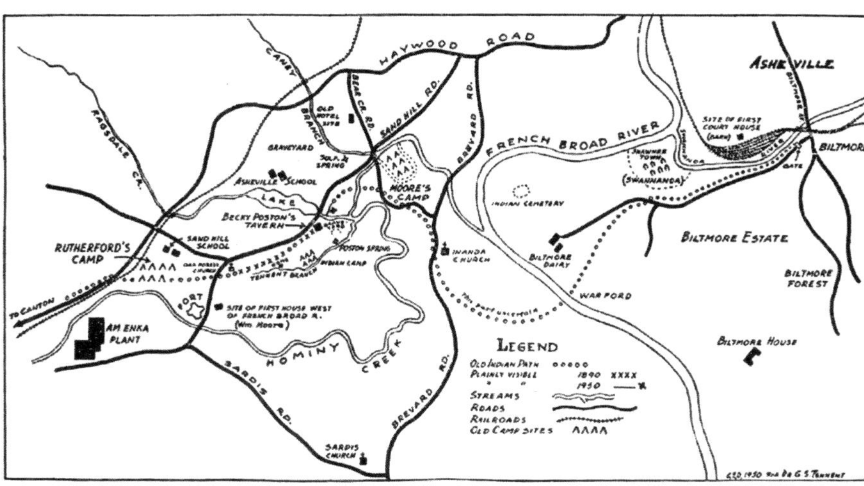

Map depicting the old Indian path and location of the Rutherford and Moore encampments. Taken from *The Indian Path in Buncombe County*, by Gaillard Tennent. *North Carolina Collection, Pack Memorial Public Library, Asheville, NC.*

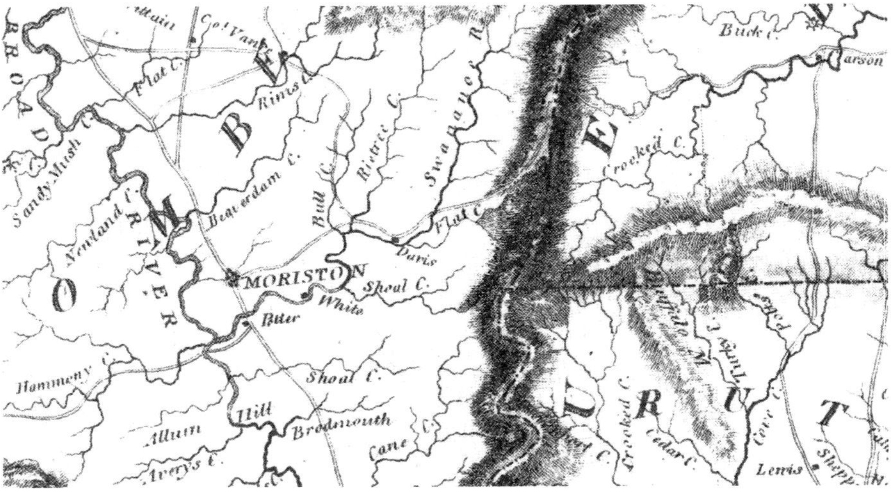

Asheville was first named Morristown, as noted on this 1808 Price-Strother map. *North Carolina Collection, Pack Memorial Public Library, Asheville, NC.*

Davidson entered for several land grants in November 1790 in association with Joseph Henry, and a land transfer deed dated April 1792 from William Davidson and Joseph Henry to David Miller was acknowledged and ordered to be registered in Buncombe County court. Joseph was a legal resident of Lincoln County at that time, but by July, deed records indicate he was a resident of Buncombe County, evidencing Joseph may have relocated to Buncombe County between April and July of 1792.

On January 25, 1792, another Joseph Henry sold James Leeper eighty-one acres in Lincoln County. It is not clear which Joseph this is, although he could be Robert's brother, as the deed was proved by Robert Henry and James Leeper, who married Robert's sister Margaret. This Joseph Henry also would leave for Buncombe County.

The first Joseph Henry, Robert's cousin, has a large presence in early court records. In January 1793, he appears in Buncombe County as Joseph Henry, Esq., recording a livestock mark and brand. In July of that year, he was appointed one of the election supervisors, and in July of the following year, he was elected as an entry taker.[59] At some point, he served as coroner for the county, an office from which he resigned in July 1798. In April 1805, he was appointed a commissioner "for the purpose of procuring a public square, from the lot, or landholders, in the town of Asheville, most convenient and interesting to the public, and least injurious to individuals, that the nature of the case will admit of."

Robert Henry followed Joseph into western North Carolina. In 1790, William Forster II purchased 640 acres of land lying on both sides of the Swannanoa from William and James Davidson. On this land, sometime before 1793, the first school west of the Blue Ridge was established, and Robert Henry, now in his mid-twenties, became the first teacher.

The log schoolhouse operated on a subscription basis and was located about a half-mile above the Swannanoa River settlement on present-day Biltmore Avenue. Known as the Union Hill School, it was attended by both boys and girls.[60] It was later formally established as Union Hill Academy, with Joseph Henry acting as one of the trustees. Perhaps Joseph had a job waiting for Robert when the school was originally established. Robert taught at the pioneer school until 1797, when he resigned and was succeeded by George Newton.[61]

In 1803, William Forster III (Jr.) deeded eight acres of his land to the trustees of Union Academy, including Robert Henry's school, as a gift for "maintenance of the gospel, and teaching a Latin or English school, or either." Union Hill Academy was removed in 1809. A new brick building took its place, and the name was changed by an act of the legislature to Newton Academy. In 1857 or 1858, this brick building "between the present academy and the graveyard was removed and the brick academy now there was erected."[62]

During his tenure at Union Hill, an incident related by granddaughter Kate Boyles occurred that Robert would long remember.[63] One day while instructing the class, a young girl by the name of Rebecca or Rhoda Alexander was in violation of some rule. Miss Alexander was called to the front of the class. This is where Robert would inflict the embarrassing and possibly painful reprimand of striking the palm of her hand with his ruler. The young lady put forth her hand to receive her punishment, but when Robert took hold of it, there was an unexpected result. Instead of taking her just due, Miss Alexander seized teacher Henry by the queue of his hair, spun him around the room and then left for home. Robert recounted this incident for as long as he lived.

Chapter 6

Running a Line

At the head of the round-about on the Stone Mountain...
our bark camp was soon fixed.

Six months after Tennessee was accepted as the sixteenth state in the Union, North Carolina passed legislation providing for the determination of an accurate western boundary line. Commissioners were appointed in December 1796 to meet with those from Tennessee to formulate guidelines for establishment of the line.

In May 1799, because the Tennessee legislature failed to appoint its commissioners, North Carolina began its own boundary survey. General Joseph McDowell, Major Mussendine Matthews and Colonel David Vance were appointed North Carolina commissioners. These were men with distinguished military service in the War for Independence. Joseph McDowell was a leader of North Carolina troops at the battle of Kings Mountain and an early settler in Buncombe County. Mussendine Matthews had been an officer in the Revolutionary War. David Vance, also one of the first in Buncombe County, was a captain at Kings Mountain and had previously served with George Washington.

By law, the commissioners received forty shillings per day for their services and were empowered by the state to employ "such surveyor or surveyors and such chain carriers and markers as they, or a majority of them, shall deem necessary."[64]

Robert Henry and John Strother were appointed the official surveyors. Strother was considerably experienced, having surveyed and mapped hundreds of thousands of acres in southeastern North Carolina.[65] He kept detailed journal records of the expedition. Since surveyors were officers of the state, their appointment was closely regulated. Henry and Strother were paid a wage of thirty shillings for every day running and marking the line. Their chain carriers and markers were allotted twenty shillings per day.

When and where Robert studied surveying is not clear. His earliest known survey was near the west bank of the Catawba River in 1795. Francis Beatty, a neighbor and cousin of Robert's father, had been a surveyor in Virginia for several years and continued surveying when he came to North Carolina.[66] Francis died in 1773, leaving his surveying equipment to his son, Robert Beatty, who would later be Robert Henry's schoolmaster and fellow battle mate. Robert Beatty died from wounds inflicted at the Battle of Cowan's Ford in February 1781, and his equipment went to his brother Hugh. Perhaps Robert studied and learned the profession at an early age from one of the Beatty family.

Surveyors enjoyed the status and respectability similar to that given a lawyer, but theirs was a much more physically demanding profession. Consider the plight of a surveyor. At the dawn of the eighteenth century, he

> *had to have an iron constitution, boundless energy, and an abundance of health. Generally, he was a man of rough and ready ways who was capable of living without the company of other people for months at a time. He responded to the challenge of the wilds and was intrigued by the mystery of unknown lands that stretched endlessly in all directions. Accounts of hardships and hazards are buried in field books of early surveyors and in letters to their loved ones. Often, when their provisions had run out or were lost in the course of their difficult travel, they were forced to subsist on the raw flesh of game or even resort to sacrificing their own mules for food. Working in virgin forests, they constantly faced threats from wildlife.*[67]

Assembling a team to conduct a boundary survey was an enormous undertaking.[68] In addition to surveyors, a host of other personnel was essential: an axe crew to clear through trees and thick underbrush, skilled hunters, a cook or commissary to prepare meals from on-board supplies and the fresh game killed by the hunters, chain bearers and markers to assist the surveyors and general laborers for menial tasks. Guides familiar with the local landscape were essential at various points along the way, and healthy and strong packhorses were required to carry supplies.

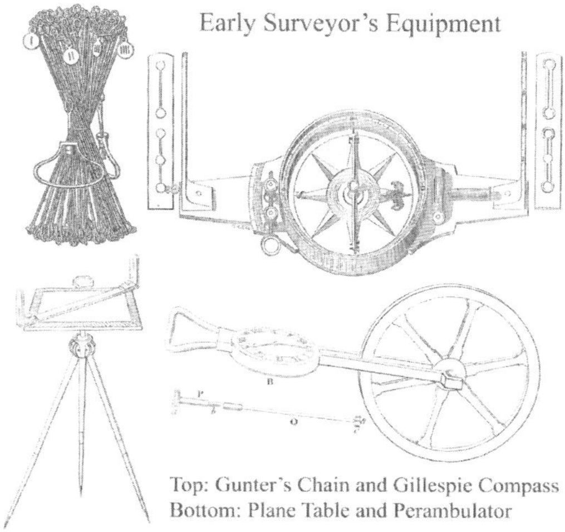

Examples of surveyor's equipment likely used by Robert Henry: Gunter's Chain, from Chain Surveying by R.J. Foster, 1930; Gillespie Compass, from A Treatise on Land Surveying, by W. M. Gillespie, 1870; Plane Table and Perambulator from Rees Cyclopedia American edition (1806-1840). *Courtesy of Surveyors Historical Society.*

American surveyors' primary tools were the plane compass, the plane table and the Gunter's chain. The plane compass was excellent in surveying in wooded regions when end points were not visible. A plane table with alidade (sighting apparatus) was used for angular measurement, and a perambulator (odometer) was useful in measuring irregular lines such as the course of a river.

The Gunter's chain, invented by English mathematician Edmund Gunter, had been in use since the 1600s. The length of the chain, based on an age-old measure of the breadth of a furrow or plough strip, was sixty-six feet, or four "poles." The chain bearers, or carriers, were instructed by the surveyor on the use of the chain and pins and did the actual measuring.

Surveying on Carolina and Tennessee mountain ridges was particularly challenging. A metal loop was attached to each end of the chain, through which was a leather strap knotted to form a loop. If the chain carrier on the top of the ridge released his grip and failed to secure the handle over a limb or other object, the chain would slide down the ridge, becoming either tangled or lying in a heap at the bottom.

Beginning in early morning, a starting marker was chosen, something easily seen that would remain for a long period of time. It might be a local resident's corner marker, or if there were none, a tree or stone could be used. The surveyor recorded a bearing from the compass and then sent the carriers chaining. While keeping an eye on the carriers, he made sure the instruments were working properly, recorded the bearings from the compass and kept detailed notes of the measurements, including a description of the corner marker. Working a good distance from each other necessitated a simple and effective method of communication. "Each party had a trumpet or horn by which we could generally find each other and the packmen, the more readily. The trumpets were carried at our backs to prevent it from interfering with the with the compass needle."[69]

On May 20, 1799, commissioners Joseph McDowell, David Vance and Mussendine Matthews; surveyors Robert Henry and John Strother (Strother did not appear at the commencement);[70] chain bearers and markers B. Collins, James Hawkins, George Penland, Robert Logan, George Davidson and John Matthews; Major James Neely, acting as commissary; two packhorse men; and a pilot (probably Gideon Lewis) camped at a waterway named Stag Creek.[71] Joined by Strother, the party set out on its expedition the next morning. Strother recorded the day in his journal:

> *21st—Set out at 8 o.c., went up Stag Creek 3 miles then ascended the ridge dividing ye water of Laurel Creek. Continued on said ridge about 7 miles to a place called the lower Rye Patch, where we refreshed ourselves till 3 o.c. p.m., then continued our route 4 miles to camp at the foot of ye Stone Mn and spent ye evening.*[72]

On May 22, surveying began "at a sugar-tree and beech on Pond Mountain, so called from two small ponds on it," at the Virginia border. Both trees are now gone, but a stone four feet by two feet and sixteen inches in thickness was buried in the ground where they stood, with a simple cross, east and west, chiseled upon it. An upper surface, level with the ground, was placed there in 1899 or 1900.

> *Friday 24th—We had but an indifferent nights rest, the wind blew extremely hard, the horses were much scattered this morning & were troublesome to find; however, they were at length collected. We eat breakfast, packed up and continued the line some miles to the head of a rich hollow, where we found good water; refreshed ourselves an hour, then set out & continued the line about ½ m when it set in and rained most powerfully, which obliged us to take up camp at the most convenient place, or rather the first place that offered as it is but at certain places where water can be had in a reasonable distance down the mountain; had a very uncomfortable wet evening.*[73]

On this night, a historic conversation took place. Knowing that several of their party had been leaders in the thick of the Kings Mountain battle, the men began asking questions regarding Ferguson's defeat and finally requested either McDowell or Vance give a connected account. Robert Henry later wrote:

> *It was agreed that Colonel Vance should give that account. The Colonel agreed to do so on consulting with McDowell, our pilot, Gideon Lewis, who had been a news-carrier, and myself* [to relate it] *on the first wet day that should happen so that we could not progress with the line. Accordingly, a wet day happened when we were at the head of the round-about on the Stone Mountain. Our bark camp was soon fixed, and Colonel Vance gave the account, ending with the details of the battle of Kings Mountain.*[74] *It was at this point Mussendine Matthews uttered a "sarcastic and sneering" remark by saying the army was "a fierce and formidable set of blue hen's chickens among eggs, if each one was provided with a stick" and that "when anybody pretends to tell the story of that transaction, it would be to his credit to play the game of shut mouth."*

Years later, Judge David Schenck suggested that Major Matthews "was either a Tory or a cynic."

General McDowell then made an "extensive reply and statement of the whole affair and its consequences." Robert Henry was given a notebook to

A "bark camp" was constructed of large pieces of bark to form the sides and roof of a small shelter, left open on one side. *From William S. Wicks's* Log Cabins: How to Build Them and Furnish Them *(1889).*

record a memorandum of events and began taking down David Vance's account. Vance said that Robert did not have the time to do it, and since he (Vance) had leisure, he would write. Vance recorded his recollections and also the reply of General McDowell to Mussendine Matthews. These recollections were referenced extensively in Lyman Draper's *Kings Mountain and Its Heroes* and were later published by David Schenck as the *Narrative of the Battle of Kings Mountain, by Captain David Vance*. Strother noted in his journal:

> *Saturday 25th—We had a very disagreeable night; the morning appears gloomy; some of our horses lost. Mr. Logan cut his foot; it will be bad. The horses were at length found; we all ate our breakfast & set out on the line went ¾ m.; it set in and rained hard and obliged to take up camp at the first place that offered, which was a br.* [branch] *of Roans creek, where we spent an uncomfortable evening; the next day being the Lords day, we spent it here in prayers for a pleasant tour to ye painted rock. Genl McDowell left us this day; he is sick.*

Gideon Lewis was not acquainted with the ridges beyond this point, so on May 28, Strother and Matthews set out in search of suitable pilots.

Colonial surveyors at work. From the Surveyors Historical Society journal *Backsights* Vol. 13, No. 1 (January 1994). *Courtesy of Surveyors Historical Society.*

Matthews went to see a Mr. Miller and the next day brought a young man back to the company. Strother returned with a Mr. Curtis. That evening, Robert Henry told Strother that Matthew's pilot "was no woodsman," so he was promptly discharged.

The survey crew continued, fighting gnats "most insufferably bad" and sometimes encountering more menacing creatures. An attempt was made to kill a very large "rattlebug" (rattlesnake), "but it was too souple [*sic*] in the heels for us."[75]

Still in need of another guide, Vance and Major James Neely went down to the Limestone Settlements and returned not only with a pilot named Mr. Collier but also with two gallons of whiskey. The men proceeded to drink to their own health and continued to run the line until evening. Camp was set on a steep "laurelly hollow," but "the whiskey had such marvelous powers that it made the place tolerably comfortable."

On rare occasions, the company enjoyed the pleasure of good food as well. For example, on a Saturday while camped near a spring, one of the hunters killed a two-year-old bear, "upon which, and some bacon stewed together with some good tea and Johnny cake, we made a Sabbath's morning breakfast fit for a European lord." Sometimes, various members of the party could go down the mountain to a nearby settlement for fresh provisions and a "good supper and a bed to sleep in."

The next morning, June 13, the new pilot informed the survey party that the line was impassable for packhorses for the next two or three days and that the horses would not be able to proceed. So Strother, the chain bearers and the markers packed their provisions on their backs and continued running the line. The rest of the company and the packhorses, led by pilot Collier, detoured around the difficult terrain via another route. Collier, too, was then found unacceptable, and on meeting back with the rest of the party on Saturday the fifteenth, he was discharged.

Continuing to the Bald Mountain, Robert Henry now carried provisions on his back while the horses were led by way of Greasy Cove. The divided party was to connect again on Sunday, the sixteenth. By Tuesday morning, another pilot had been hired. His name was Colonel Robert Love. Love was a resident of Buncombe County but had first settled at Greasy Cove in 1782, so he was familiar with the terrain. Although historian John Preston Arthur states that on this day, Robert Henry "met his fate," Henry probably already knew Love. In early court records, Love was associated with many of the same Buncombe County residents as was Robert and Joseph Henry.

The mountain expedition was becoming increasingly strenuous and difficult. By the twentieth, water was scarce, a distance from the line. The march was severe, the ground on which to camp was very steep and the gnats were still bad. The horses wandered a mile or two from camp and had to be retrieved, suffering for two days because there was no food or water.

Finally, on Saturday the twenty-second, they reached the top of Beech Mountain, where they found a good spring and sufficient range for their horses. Their grueling ordeal was finally near completion. Camp was set until the following Monday. For the next several days, the boundary was determined and set over some very high and rough Laurel and Brushy knobs. After straying off line and committing several wrong turns, camp was

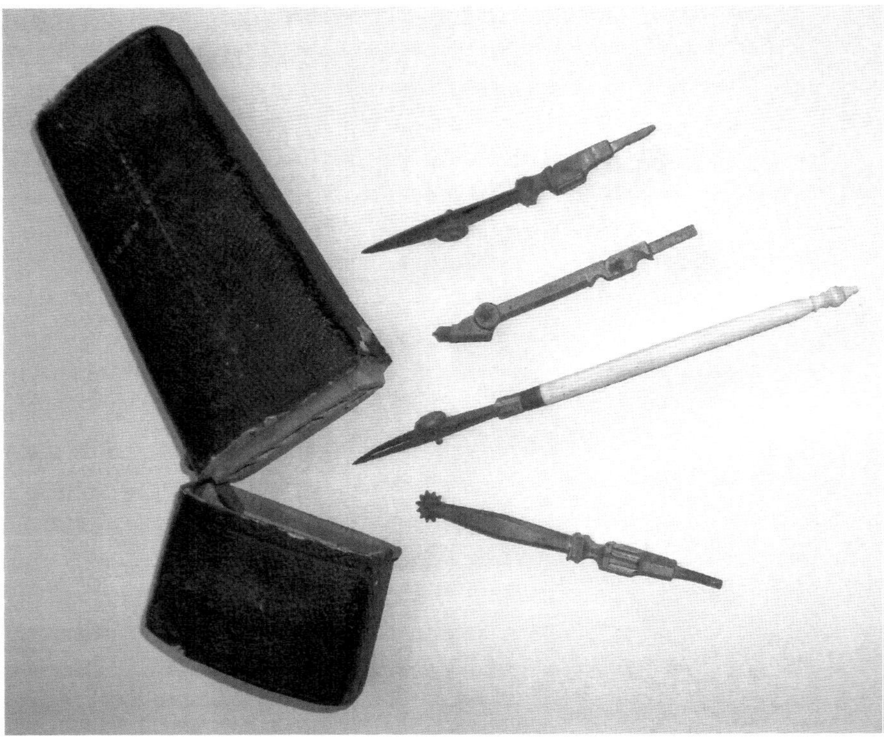

Robert Henry's drafting kit with sharkskin traveling case. *From top to bottom*: pen point attachment for dividers (missing), pencil point attachment for dividers, a drawing pen with ivory handle and adjusting attachment and a roulette pen for drawing dotted lines. Ruler and/or protractor are missing. *Henry Archive (private collection).*

A view of Paint Rock from across the French Broad River. *North Carolina Collection, Pack Memorial Public Library, Asheville, NC.*

set between the waters of the French Broad River and Paint Creek. Strother recorded the following entries:

> *Thursday 27th—This morning is cloudy & hasey* [sic]*; the commissioners, being anctoous* [sic] *to get on to the Painted rock, Started us early; went on with the line a small distance; took a wrong ridge and fell into another fork of Paint Cr.; returned and encamped on the right ridge, where we spent our time uncomfortable this evening.*
>
> *Friday 28th—Set out very early and proceeded on the line about 4 m to the Painted rock on F.B. River, about 5 m below the Warm Springs; measured the height of the rock and found it to be 107 feet 3 inches high from the top to the base; it rather projects over. The face of the rock bears but few traces of its having formerly been painted—owing to*

> *its being smoked by pine knots and other wood from a place at its base where travelers have frequently camped. In the year 1790, it was not much smoked; the pictures of some human's, wild beasts, fish & fowls were to be seen plainly made with red paint, some of them 20 & 30 feet from its base.*

On Saturday the twenty-ninth, most of the survey team returned home for a few weeks rest, while Strother stayed at the springs to "get clear of the fatigue of the tour."

Chapter 7

The Professional

In his countenance there was a sneaking craven expression, better becoming a criminal than an advocate.

Robert Henry's first Buncombe County residence was probably in the home of his cousin Joseph. He does not appear in early census records, and because only the head of household was enumerated by name, it is unknown with whom he was residing for several years. It is possible he that he stayed with family in Lincoln County for periods of time. Evidence suggests that Robert moved back to his South Fork home after teaching at Union Hill. In 1797, he witnessed several legal documents there with his brother Isaac Henry and appears in various Tryon County[76] court records. And in an 1800 land deed, he is recorded as a Lincoln County resident.

Robert excelled as both an attorney and surveyor. Another career was short-lived, however. Robert studied and practiced medicine as well. In this capacity, he was helpful throughout the local community, but when he was called upon to perform a caesarian-section birth, he recognized the profession was not for him after all.[77] A reading of his medical notes gives a colorful insight into treatment methods of the era:

> *Cholera Morbus, or Puking and Purging: I will state a case that I attended not long ago and that will give you a general view how such cases would be treated by me. Mrs. Hogan had been taken with puking and purging. She was far advanced in her complaint. She was accustomed to profuse cold sweats. She was cold in the arms and legs. The puking and purging were severe.*

> *Remedy: I discovered I could not interfere with the purging, for everything that she would take internally she immediately threw back, hence I considered in the puking must first be stopped. To effect this, I applied a plaster of mustard and proceeded to wet with warm vinegar to the pit of her stomach and at the same time applied a cloth wrung out of cold water, letting this remain about ten minutes. This stopped the puking. I then gave her a drink of strong ginger, as warm as she could drink it, to heat the stomach. She retained this. Then, about half an hour passed to stop the purging.*[78]

Historians' opinions differ regarding when and where Robert studied for his several occupations.[79] His teaching, attorney and surveyor work overlap, rendering a determination of an accurate succession of events nearly impossible. Robert had surveyed a tract of land in Lincoln County as early as 1795 while still employed as a teacher at Union Academy.[80] In January 1799, Robert worked with an attorney named Spencer in a Lincoln County court case. By May 1799, he was in the west surveying the state line.

"Reading law" with an established attorney was required before one could be accepted to practice law. When the mentor felt his student was qualified, he filed a motion in court for the apprentice to be admitted into professional practice. Robert worked with Spencer in Lincoln County either as an attorney or an apprentice. In July 1802, Spencer, who had been admitted in Buncombe County in 1794, filed an admission motion for Robert. Court records read:

> *On motion of Joseph Spencer Esquire, it is ordered that Robert Henry, Esquire, be admitted to practice as an attorney in the County Court of Buncombe, his license being produced signed by the Judges McCay & Hall and former qualification attested by John Dixon, Clerk of Lincoln County Court.*[81]

Robert has been credited as the first "resident" attorney in Buncombe County.[82]

Lawyers "rode the circuit" trying court cases in various towns, traveling the same routes as their judge counterparts. Colonel A.T. Davidson, a grandson of David Vance, stated:

> *We traveled together on horseback, stopped at the same hotels in the towns, and at the same wayside inns in the country; and it was not unusual to have ten or fifteen of us together at these country stopping places, where the wit and humor of the profession broke loose in all its force, and good*

> *humor ruled the house. It is a fact that nearly all of those mentioned were gentlemen of fine humor, and but few given to strong drink, so that the jest and humor were of the best character, without boistering or noise.*[83]

Robert, however, may have been an exception to Davidson's observations of "gentlemen." He was known to be fond of strong drink and associated not only with fellow lawyers but also with the regular citizenry and even the accused. "The rabble with whom he so freely associated, conversed, smoked, drank whiskey and slept, whose lingo he adopted and whose dress and manner he shared, were the jurors in a court where about every question was left to the determination of the jury."[84] Robert sometimes appeared in court in his bare feet.[85]

In 1826, one of the rider judges was a man by the name of Robert Strange. He rode a circuit in the western North Carolina mountains that included the court in Waynesville. Over the years, he recorded stories of the happenings of the time and his observations of people he encountered. In 1839, he published the book *Eoneguski, or, the Cherokee Chief: A Tale of Past Wars*. *Eoneguski* was the first novel written by a native of North Carolina depicting the events and the inhabitants of that state. The novel, sympathetic to the plight of Native Americans, did not do well at the time.[86]

Strange believed that North Carolina lawyers were of a different class. Their training was unlike their English counterparts, but they were nonetheless highly competent. While those in established eastern sections of the state dressed in fine, fashionable clothes and traveled over the level plains, perhaps with a servant, their mountain brother "jogs along, over hill and valley, and sometimes scaling the side of a precipice, with his time-worn and well-filled saddlebags flapping against the sides of his horse."[87]

Although considered a work of fiction, Strange's characters were based on real individuals he met during his travels. The principal white character was drawn from Robert Love, and the story included an old lawyer named "Mr. Johns," modeled after Robert Henry.[88] Several mountain lawyers were gathered in Waynesville, seeking business and cases to plead in court, Mr. Johns among them. Because the village proprietors knew their schedules and had provided food and board many times previous, accommodations were waiting for the visitors on their arrival. The innkeepers knew what to expect. "I am afraid we shall have our hands full of drunkards tonight," said Mrs. Holland to her husband. "I suppose Smoothly and Rowell will both come home tipsy, as usual, and old Johns will not be far behind them." Robert Strange elaborated extensively on his description of Johns (Robert Henry):

> *Mr. Johns is, by right of seniority, first entitled to consideration amongst them. He was a tall lank man, about fifty years of age, with locks originally black, thickly sprinkled with gray. In his countenance there was a sneaking craven expression, better becoming a criminal than an advocate, and yet it was in the defence of criminals, strange as it may seem, he had attained a proud pre-eminence in all the courts he attended.*
>
> *A stranger would have taken him for the humblest of the bumpkins who hovered about the bar; and when he opened his mouth, its harsh and unmusical tones would never have suggested, that in them dwelt the notes of soft persuasion. But when he witnessed the sad sufferings of the English language in the throat, palate, tongue, and beautiful teeth of Mr. Johns, as it was slowly and stammeringly uttered, he would wonder still more wherein lay his resemblance to the fecund Mercury.*
>
> *And a yet higher flight would await his astonishment when he looked upon his mean countenance—his bleared lack-lustre eyes—the graceless stoop of his shoulders—his open collar, exposing a scraggy neck, from which the* pomum adami *protruded like a large wen—his slovenly ill-arranged clothing—and his spindle shanks appearing beneath his pantaloons, a world too short as well as too wide, and exposing their nakedness (for they always disdained, except in the severest weather, the comfort of a stocking).*
>
> *And yet this man, having neither the gait, air, action, nor utterance of a Christian, was certainly a successful criminal advocate, nay, even bore away the palm from all competition—but by "what charms, what conjuration, or what magic" he won his causes, withal, is perhaps a professional secret. He usually occupied no place within the bar, and save when actually engaged in the management of a cause, might be seen mingling with the people of the court-yard, until his social habits had stretched him (which was frequently the case) upon the bed of penitence.*

Following a long day in court, the colleagues returned to the inn for the evening. Regardless of the arguments and outcomes of their legal debates during the day, the men "were exceedingly free and easy in their intercourse with each other out of court." The boarders were wondering what could be considered a valid excuse to wash down the day's work with a drink when old Johns, in an accented voice, said:

> *Well boys, I am like the feller who, hearing one cry out for licker bekase he was cold, and another bekase he was warm, called to the waiter, "Bring me*

> *a glass of brandy and water, bekase I likes it." So Holland, do let me have something to drink, bekase I likes it.*

The merriment continued until late at night, when proprietor Holland and Mr. Johns, smoking their pipes, began commenting on the conversation of the others in attendance:

> *"Well," said old Johns, "happy to find the conversation once more coming back to plain everyday English; what Smoothly says puts me in mind of the old story of the kettle calling the pot black; come, both of you, drap it like a hot potato, and let Smoothly give us a song. Father Holland, you have no objections to Mr. Smoothly's giving us a song; it won't disturb the family, will it?"*
>
> *"I can't sing at all," said Smoothly. "I feel that infernal tobacco juice in my throat this minute; besides, I have a cold, and my voice, Johns, is nearly as much cracked as your own."*
>
> *"I thank you for the compliment," replied Johns, "if not for your great willingness to oblige. I never saw one of your rale singers that was worth a pipe of tobacco; they are sartain to have a cold, if a man axes them to sing; and when nobody cares about hearing them, they are eternally singing or whistling, like the wind through the key-hole of a winter night."*

Despite the unflattering but believed accurate portrayal by Strange, Henry was very well respected in his profession. Colonel A.T. Davidson stated:

> *I must not omit...to mention Robert Henry, who lived, owned and settled the Sulphur Springs. He was an old man when I first knew him, say fifty years ago. He had then retired from the profession of the law which he had practiced many years. This was before I knew him well. He was tedious and slow in conversation, but always interesting to the student. He had been a fine lawyer, and remarkable in criminal cases. He could recite his experiences of cases in most minute detail. He insisted that, underlying all, there was invariably a principle which settled every rule of evidence and point of law. I chanced to get some of his old criminal law books, such as Foster's Crown Law, Hale's Pleas of the Crown, etc., and I found them well annotated with accurate marginal notes, showing great industry and thought in their perusal.*[89]

Robert held many official positions as an attorney. In 1804, he was clerk and master of equity for the Superior Court of Equity in the Morgan

District.[90] The Morgan District included the counties of Burke, Wilkes, Rutherford, Lincoln and Buncombe. The court met on the first day of March and September in Morgan Town (Morganton). As "C.M.&E.," Robert's duties included recording the proceedings of the court and bills, answers and decrees and documenting them in a bound book. He was authorized to administer the oath to witnesses and to others who came before the court.[91] He held this position for several years, at least through March 1807.

In January 1806, apparently while still C.M.&E. in the Morgan District, Robert was appointed as solicitor, or prosecuting attorney, for Buncombe County.[92] Court records, legal advertisements and personal notebook entries indicate Robert continued as solicitor until February 1811. For two meetings of the court, one in July 1807 and one in July 1810, a temporary solicitor was appointed in his absence. Robert was practicing as a defense attorney in July 1812, when John Paxton replaced him as solicitor.[93]

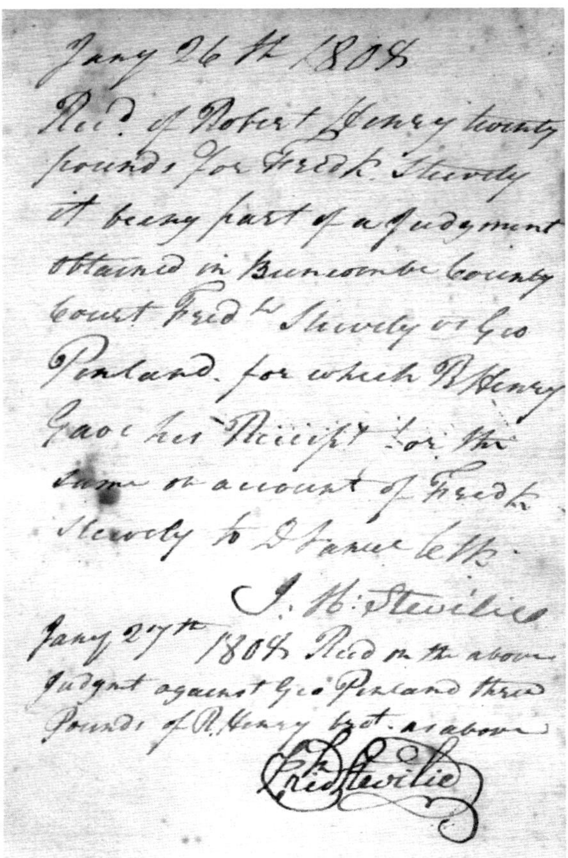

Jany 26th 1808
Recd of Robert Henry twenty pounds for Fredk Steevly it being part of a Judgment obtained in Buncombe County Court Fredk Steevely vs Geo Penland. for which R Henry Gave his Receipt for the same on account of Fredk Steevly to D Vance Clk.
J. M. Stevilie
Jany 27th 1808 Recd on the above Judgmt against Geo Penland three Pounds of R Henry Esqr. as above
Fred Stevilie

Robert Henry, acting as Buncombe County solicitor, paid Frederick Stevilie twenty pounds collected from an 1808 court case. The clerk of court is David Vance. *Henry Archive (private collection).*

In 1806, the North Carolina legislature enacted a bill stating that "a Superior Court shall be held at the courthouse in each county in the state twice every year." The state was divided into six circuits, one being Buncombe, where the first Buncombe County Superior Court was held in March of 1807.[94] Robert became clerk of the Superior Court of Buncombe County, his signature appearing on several 1819 deeds. A newspaper legal advertisement placed on March 23, 1824, indicates that he was still serving as Buncombe County clerk during the fall term of 1823.[95]

At some point in his career, Robert became a defender of the accused. He is recorded in court documents as an attorney in Lincoln County in 1809, 1811 and 1812. In at least one of those cases, he was the defending attorney. Robert reportedly tried sixty-three cases as a defense lawyer, losing just three, of which only two of his clients were punished.[96] One such case was the *State v. William Tolliver*, which began in March 1811 in the Superior Court of Ashe County, North Carolina. Robert was the defending attorney for Tolliver, who was charged with the murder of George Reeves Jr.

It is speculated that Tolliver killed Reeves because Reeves had attempted liberties with his wife. However, family tradition holds that Mr. Reeves, a tax collector, was taking horses for taxes when Tolliver mistook him for a horse thief and shot and killed him.[97]

When the trial was moved to Wilkes County court, Ashe County officials were ordered to "procure a sufficient guard of eight men from the proper officers of the militia to convey safely the said William Tolliver to the Superior Court of Wilkes County."[98] But there was fear of an escape or lynching. The jail was "insecure," so Tolliver was to be sent instead to the jail in Salisbury until the sheriff of Wilkes, or his deputy, should call for him.[99]

On September 18 and 19, 1811, the trial was continued, and on the twentieth, a jury verdict was rendered. Tolliver was found not guilty of murder but was guilty of manslaughter. He was sentenced to be burned with the letter "M" on the brawn of the left thumb, confined to jail for three years until he could give security for his good behavior and fined the sum of £1,000.

In an unpublished footnote of F.A. Sondley's biography of Henry, it is claimed that the second of his clients to receive punishment was Frankie Silver. Silver was convicted of murdering and dismembering her husband and was hanged in 1833. Sondley's source is not stated, however, and although he may have been involved, there is no mention of Henry in court documents.

Chapter 8

Husband and Traveler

Robert Henry was married to Dorcas B. Love on the 31st day of May 1814.

Robert began speculating in land at a very young age. In September 1786, he and another Kings Mountain veteran, Joseph Dobson, filed for a Buncombe County land grant of 300 acres on the north fork of Jonathon's Creek, located near Waynesville, North Carolina. In 1790, Robert filed for a Buncombe County land grant of 200 acres on Bolin's Creek on the waters of the Caney River and, in 1794, for 200 acres on Erwin's Creek above the mouth of Robinson's Creek. Another filing was made in 1794 for 250 acres on Crystal Creek of the Big Pigeon River.[100]

In 1800, Robert entered a claim for two hundred acres on Erwin's Creek in Buncombe County. Records reveal that several more filings totaling more than one thousand acres along the French Broad River and Little Willow Creek were made over the next year. One of those entries was a joint claim with Joseph Henry for five hundred acres adjoining Joseph's lands. It is not clear if this was Robert's brother Joseph or the early settler and cousin known as "Entry Taker Joe." In September 1808, Robert surveyed some of his own land grants, including two he had filed jointly with Joseph Henry in 1801.

Land claims and boundary lines were commonly marked with a prominent landmark or by initialing trees. At least two of the abovementioned claims were identified by carving the initials "R.H." in chestnut and hickory trees. Known as "tomahawk rights," a settler often deadened some trees near a spring and engraved the bark with his name or initials. This method was generally recognized by the settlers, but it did not give the claimant legal title

An example of marking boundary lines, this "H" was found carved in a tree located on a corner of Robert Henry's homestead near Hominy Creek. *Photo by author.*

unless he secured the warrant and patent from the land office or physically occupied the land. Sometimes, a tomahawk right was purchased from the original applicant to avoid future disputes.[101]

In the twenty years following his first claim, Robert entered for at least two thousand acres in several North Carolina counties and in middle and western Tennessee. He traveled to Tennessee multiple times over the decades, attending to land purchases, sales and other legal issues. Between the March and September 1811 sessions of the Morgan Court, Robert made his first recorded journey to the "Western Country" in the company of an old friend and neighbor, Dr. William MacLean (or McLean).

Robert and MacLean had much in common. They had both been residents in the South Point area near the South Fork of the Catawba River, and both were veterans of Kings Mountain—Robert a volunteer soldier, and William a "surgeon's mate" in the Continental Army. Following the Battle of Kings Mountain, MacLean attended medical school in Philadelphia, afterward returning home and purchasing a farm near the South Fork.[102] In 1815, he purchased, erected and had dedicated the first commemorative marker for Kings Mountain, honoring the Lincoln County men who perished in the fight.

MacLean left his home near the South Fork on May 12, 1811, heading northwest, first stopping to outfit in Lincolnton.[103] Following the Morganton Road to the one leading through the Whitesides settlement (now beneath Lake Lure), he continued toward the headwaters of the Catawba River in the mountains and to the crest of the Blue Ridge. After several days away from home, he descended the western slopes of the Blue Ridge. On May 15, MacLean wrote his wife and informed her that he "called upon Mr. Samuel Davidson and his lady, with whom I was obliged to stay and take breakfast." The Davidson family living in the "Swannanoa Settlement" near Bee Tree Creek was probably kin to MacLean's wife, Mary Davidson. He continued, "From this to Asheville 10 miles, arrived at Major Erwin's in this place eleven o'clock. Found Mr. Henry and agreed to set out in Co. tomorrow." MacLean noted they both had business in Knoxville, as well as near Richland Creek in Davidson County, Tennessee, where the Joneses lived, and that it was probable they would return together.

Following the Revolution, Continental soldiers or their heirs were eligible to receive bounty lands in Tennessee as a reward for their service. To receive title for public land, a veteran must have obtained a warrant for the land or purchased a warrant from another. A warrant indicated the number of acres granted but did not give the physical location of the property. The task of locating the land fell to the warrantee, who then was required to have it recorded by an entry taker, surveyed and platted. Once this was done, he submitted the survey and plat to the Tennessee secretary of state, who issued the grant.

MacLean wished to find 2,500 acres in western Tennessee he had received for services as surgeon and have it surveyed. Henry was an assignee of several Tennessee grants and needed to locate these lands as well.

At 7:30 a.m. the next morning, the pair left Asheville, heading north on a primitive road paralleling the French Broad River known in later years as the Drover's Road and the Buncombe Turnpike. Travel along this route was difficult and dangerous. Steep mountain outcroppings sometimes lined the river so closely that "side fords" had to be taken within the waters of the French Broad. During times of high water, many of these side fords were impassable.

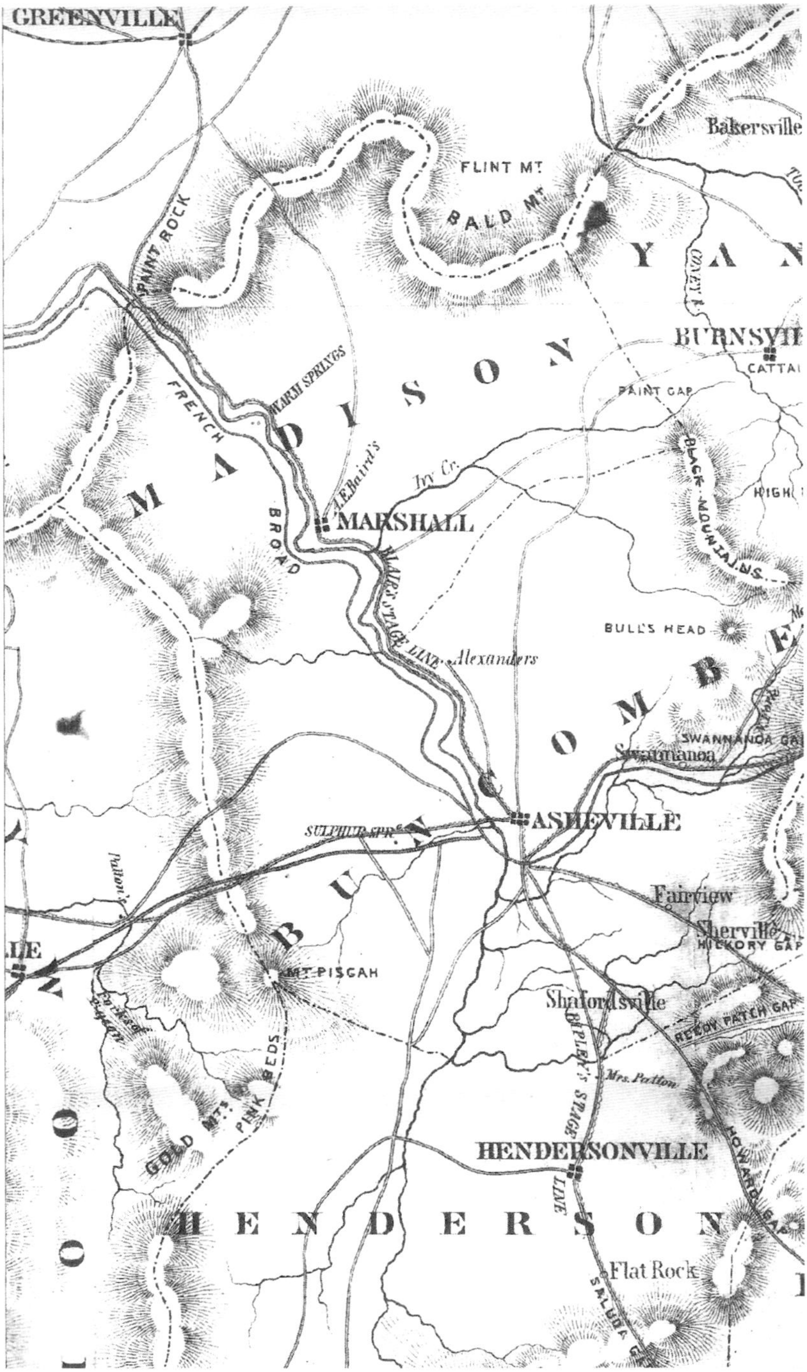

Portion of an early western North Carolina map with the Buncombe Turnpike paralleling the French Broad River. From Henry Colton's *Mountain Scenery* (1859). *North Carolina Collection, Pack Memorial Public Library, Asheville, NC.*

Hack taking the side ford on the French Broad River. *North Carolina Collection, Pack Memorial Public Library, Asheville, NC.*

The turnpike from Asheville to Warm Springs is "directly on the brink of the rapid and agitated river, often within its former bed, and so narrow as in many places to be impassable for two carriages at a time. On your right rises an almost perpendicular bank, covered with large trees clustered with vines, and here and there overhang the road, tremendous rocks, whose balance apparently an infant might destroy and send tumbling down on all below. When you have reached the springs or returned to Asheville, you feel like you had awoke from a terrific dream, in which you had escaped some indescribable danger, and the calm, which succeeds this storm of feeling, is as great as contrast can make it."[104]

Arriving at Barnett's Station and paying a turnpike toll of twenty-five cents, MacLean and Henry continued to Warm Springs (now Hot Springs).

Rocks overhang the road along the French Broad River, circa 1880. *North Carolina Collection, Pack Memorial Public Library, Asheville, NC.*

From there, they boarded in succession several ferries crossing waterways to Newport, Tennessee, forded the Big Pigeon River and went on to Dandridge in Jefferson County. Ferrying the Holston River, they made their way to Knoxville, now five days into their journey. From there, they went on to Kingston and westward, turning south off the main road for the Sequatchie Valley along the ridges of the Cumberland Mountains.

Fording the French Broad River at Alexander's. *North Carolina Collection, Pack Memorial Public Library, Asheville, NC.*

At the foot of the western Cumberlands, horse feeding, breakfast and a half-pint of whiskey set them back seventy-five cents. MacLean's journal states that they went "to Enock Jobs, 12 miles, road hilly and part of it barren, otherwise very good. Horses fed here cost 25 cents. May 23 at noon, parted with Mr. Henry half a mile from Jobs. He took the Elk River road, I the Nashville Road."

The Elk River in Lincoln County, Tennessee, flows through land ceded in 1806 by the Cherokee and Chickasaw. Robert had been assigned a grant of three hundred acres on a southern branch of the Elk by James Patton and Andrew Erwin.

By June 2, MacLean reached his destination in Robertson County, where he supervised the survey of his grant by Henry Johnston. He arrived back in North Carolina around June 20, but Robert may not have returned with him as he had planned. Robert was not present for the July session of the Buncombe County court, and a temporary solicitor had been appointed in his absence.[105] However, he was home by September 1811 for the conclusion of the murder case of William Tolliver.

In the next few years, Robert obtained more grants in Lincoln and Madison Counties, Tennessee, and in Buncombe County, North Carolina, and sold some of his holdings on the Elk River, as well as on the Pigeon River in North Carolina.

In addition to his relationship with MacLean, Robert kept in close touch with other friends as well, some of whom were now in public service and positions of power. He had a keen interest in national and state affairs and politics. He exchanged letters with an old associate and attorney named Israel Pickens, who was then serving in the United States House of Representatives. Pickens and Robert had worked legal cases in Buncombe County and Lincoln County courts.[106] Pickens was admitted to the Buncombe County Bar in 1805.[107] In 1821, he became governor of Alabama. In 1812 and 1813, their letters discussed local and national politics and deteriorating British-American relations. In a letter to Henry dated December 16, 1812, Pickens mentioned the possibility of Robert raising a military company during the War of 1812.

Robert Love, whom Henry had known as one of the pilots when he was surveying the state boundary line, and probably from their early days in Buncombe County, had founded and was living in the town of Waynesville, North Carolina. Love's daughter, Dorcas Bell, was seventeen. Henry, now forty-seven, likely had known Dorcas since the day she was born. On May 31, 1814, he and Dorcas Bell Love were married.

> *Robert Henry was married to Dorcas B. Love on the 31st day of May 1814 and took up housekeeping at Jarrett's place the 18th* [of] *November.*

In November, the couple made their home near Hominy Creek on land owned by John Jarrett. Dorcas's brother, John Love, was boarding with them, reading law with Robert.[108] In August 1815, Robert purchased the home and 100 adjoining acres from Jarrett, and in December, he purchased another 640 acres lying on both sides of Hominy Creek from neighbor Thomas Jones. Acquiring another 30 acres, he now owned 770 acres for his homestead for a total investment of $1,200.[109] The Henrys remained on their Jarrett land until December 1816, when they moved onto the land purchased from Thomas Jones.

> [During] *the summer of 1815, no rain fell from the 8th of July to the 8th of September. Trees died.*

Married and settled in his new home, Robert continued his practice of buying and selling land. On January 7, 1819, the United States Senate ratified a

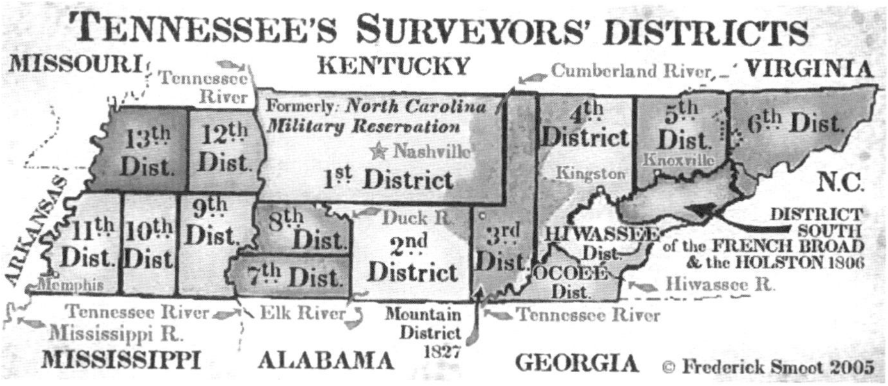

Robert Henry traveled several times to middle and western Tennessee. Map of Tennessee's early surveyor's districts. *Tennessee GenWeb Project.*

treaty with the Chickasaw, whereby for the sum of $300,000, the Chickasaw ceded all lands east of the Mississippi River and north of the Mississippi state line. Surveyor's districts seven through thirteen were established in west Tennessee by the Tennessee Assembly. The sales office was to be located in Nashville.

Most soldiers who received warrants did not go to the Western Country to claim them. Commonly, they sold their claims to speculators for a small fee, or payment would be a portion of the bounty land, given to the assignee for his services in locating the claim.[110] Robert was off to Tennessee once again. Leaving his wife, children and farm, he returned to "West Tennessee" at least twice in the next two years, traveling to the Forked Deer river. His intention was to locate and claim several warrants assigned to him by Revolutionary War veterans.

> *On the first of November 1819, I started to the Forked Deer in the Chickesaw purchase.*

During the next two years, over 5,000 acres in Tennessee were assigned to Henry by Joseph Dickson, Charles Williamson, John Armstrong, the heirs of Alexander Coles and the heirs of William Chronicle.[111] Because Chronicle held the rank of captain, he received a grant of 3,840 acres. Henry had witnessed the death of Chronicle at Kings Mountain. James McKee, Chronicle's half-brother and only legal heir, assigned his warrant to Henry.

Henry succeeded in locating the Chronicle tract, either personally or with the aid of his "locator," relative William C. Love, and completed all steps

Imagine Robert Henry heading home after a long journey. Traveler on the French Broad. *North Carolina Collection, Pack Memorial Public Library, Asheville, NC.*

required to obtain the grant. Love was paid for his service with 274 acres, worth fifty cents per acre, and some apple trees in North Carolina. Robert returned home by March 1820.

In August 1820, a warrant was issued for an 1819 contract to procure Revolutionary War land warrants for John Long, one half of which would go to Henry and a man named Burton. In October, Henry again traveled west, returning home in February 1821.

In 1856, Henry was not yet in possession of the official grant documents for the Chronicle tract he located in 1819. It would now be his son William's task to take care of business. Robert wrote detailed instructions to William explaining how he may locate the land and papers.[112] Samuel Wilson, the principal surveyor of District No. 9, had a quarrel with his deputy surveyors regarding his portion of the surveyor's fees. Robert explained that by "caveat or some light proceedings," Wilson had obtained an injunction interdicting the force of any grants issued until he received payment. Robert's Chronicle land was among those grants affected.

Robert had seen the deputy surveyor's receipts among the papers of William C. Love, and the bounds of the tract had been entered in the book of entries in order that James Bright could enter them on the general plat of the district. Mr. Bright, the "mathematician," should be able to tell William where the papers may be found, or perhaps, Robert suggested, the grant had been issued and was lying in some office somewhere or among the papers of Love.

William successfully completed his father's wishes. Writing from Fayetteville, Tennessee, on May 29, 1856, he asked his wife to "say to Papa the District land can be secured." Robert willed approximately two thousand acres of this land "on the waters of the Middle Fork of the Forked Deer in Henderson County, known by the name of the Pinson tract," to grandson Robert P. Tidwell.

[Slave] *Julia's child John was born* [on the] *6th* [of] *February 1823.*

Chapter 9

Sulphur Springs

I discovered the Sulphur Springs the last of February 1827.

Robert Henry was living a remarkable life, one full of risk, accomplishment and adventure. By 1827, he had witnessed historic deliberations, been injured in the war for America's independence, educated the children of pioneers and heroes, surveyed wilderness lands and traveled frequently. Through his surveying, business and legal careers, Robert accumulated considerable net worth. In 1828, he was able to co-sign a $10,000 bond for John B. Love when Love became clerk of Haywood County Superior Court of Law.[113] He amassed thousands of acres of prime real estate in North Carolina and Tennessee. In 1830, he appeared on the tax list for Lincoln County, Tennessee, as owner of over 1,300 acres near the Elk River alone.

He served as solicitor of Buncombe County, clerk and master of equity for the Superior Court of Equity in Morgan District and clerk of Buncombe County Superior Court of Law. In 1822, he was chosen as a member of the Committee of Correspondence representing Buncombe County in the call for a North Carolina constitutional convention.[114]

Robert was married at forty-seven, an age when most men already had adult children and probably a number of grandchildren, but Robert's family was young and included a toddler of less than twelve months. Henry's children in 1827 were Mary Louise, born September 3, 1815; Elizabeth Isabella, born May 12, 1818;[115] Robert Marcellus, born February 10, 1821; William Lewis, born November 24, 1823; and Martha Ann, born June 29, 1826.

View of Asheville from Beaucatcher Mountain, 1851. *North Carolina Collection, Pack Memorial Public Library, Asheville, NC.*

Robert and Dorcas Bell's residence had been at the "Joneses Place" since 1816.[116] Dorcas tended to the household and their growing family, while Robert oversaw and worked to improve the operation of his plantation, which now included orchards, vegetable gardens, fields of grain and many head of livestock. One of his improvements was a labor-saving device described by neighbor Mary Gudger Moore:

> *Robert Henry...was very fond of small hominy,* [and he] *devised a plan whereby he could have it beaten without physical labor. He put his corn in a mortar at the foot of a hill and swung a pestle above it to a pole turning on a pivot and the other end attached to an open box or tray under a spout of water carried down the hill. When this box or tray was full, it fell with a thud, and the pestle went up. When the water spilled out, the pole went up and the pestle down, cracking the corn. This was kept up all day, and his hominy was ready for his supper and breakfast. After a while, he began to miss his corn and thought someone was stealing it; so he watched and found an old cow that roamed at large by it. He had learned to time his head to the motion of the pestle and when it went up, thrust it in and took a mouth full and drew it out before it came down. In this way, he had eaten up his corn.*[117]

Moore also wrote that Robert was "inclined to solve the mysteries of nature" and "studied the habits of the wild animals and insects." Perhaps it was during one of his investigative outdoor explorations, the last of February

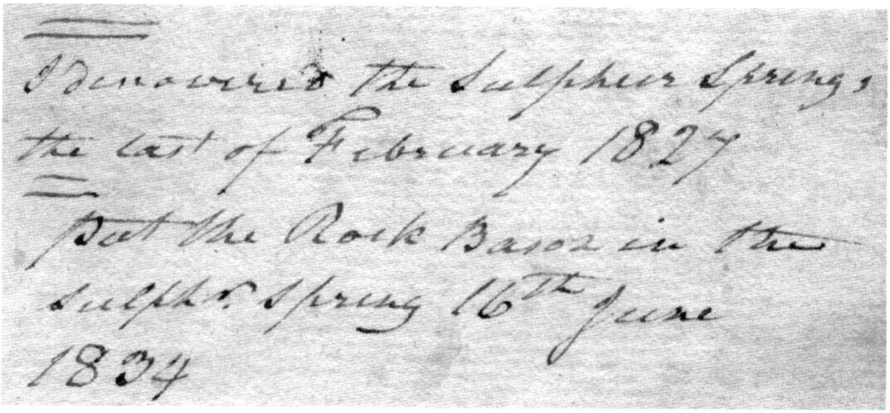

I discovered the Sulphur Springs the last of February 1827
Put the Rock Bason in the Sulphr Spring 16th June 1834

The discovery of the Sulphur Springs was a catalyst for early tourism in the Asheville area. *Henry Archive (private collection).*

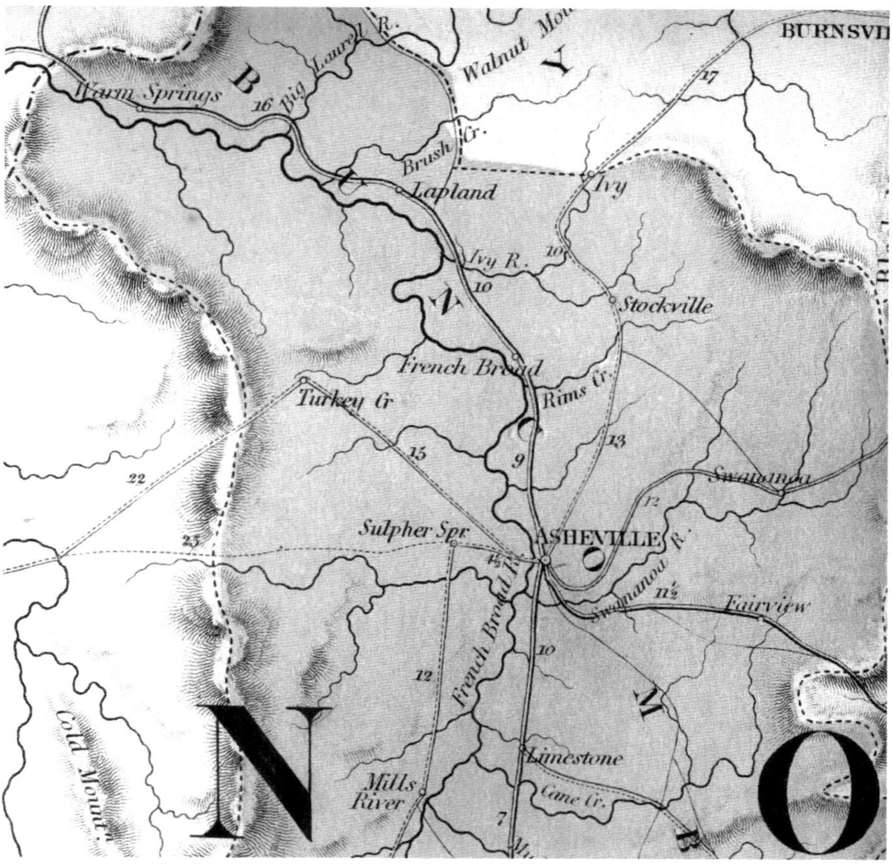

Sulphur Springs appeared on David H. Burr's 1839 map of the Carolinas. *North Carolina Collection, Pack Memorial Public Library, Asheville, NC.*

1827, when he came to discover several naturally occurring springs bubbling near the bank of Caney Creek, a small tributary emptying into Hominy Creek. Although a journal entry mentions only Henry as the discoverer, it has been written that he was accompanied by a slave known as Buncombe Sam—or even that Sam was the sole discoverer. One of these springs had a distinct although slight odor of rotten eggs and became known as the "Sulphur Springs."[118]

Robert realized the springs were potentially an important part of his plantation. Surrounded by wetlands, he began having them cleared and drained with strategically placed trenches. Swamp areas were "ditched" from the location of the springs to within approximately sixty yards of the old Haywood Road, now Smoky Park Highway.

Robert suffered a temporary setback when fire consumed his home, the "Joneses Place," on April 1, 1828. Later that year or early in 1829, a new house was built about a quarter of a mile from the spring. Carpenter Alexander Henry was employed to build the frame home and was assisted by Robert's slave Jack.[119] The house stood for many years, and in the 1850s, it served as the home of Robert's son William.

In January 1829, Robert hired neighbor John Jarrett to manage the farm for the year. Although Robert had begun his own improvements, they were more than he could handle, and Jarrett found the farm's overall condition in decline. The property was generally run down and in disrepair. Fencing was poor, with sections rotted, and could not be depended upon to protect a crop. The grounds were not kept up, and the land was worn out. The wet areas around the springs Robert had cleared and ditched were returning to swamp land. Jarrett began the sorely needed repairs and took action to improve production. Fences were mended, and worn-out farmlands were replenished by manuring. Corn and oats were planted and hay harvested for the horses.

> [On the] *2nd day of June 1829, we moved from Joneses old place to our new frame house.*

In September 1829, Jarrett was sent to see Dillard Love, a son of Robert Love, living in Waynesville. His mission was to bring back a slave girl named Hannah, then seven or eight years old. Jarrett brought her back to the Henry household, where her function was to be the "waiting girl on Mrs. Henry." She remained the property of Mrs. Henry until 1856, when she was transferred by Mrs. Henry's will to daughter Martha A. Arthur.

Three years after the discovery of the springs, a marriage took place that influenced the course of history for the Henry land, Sulphur Springs and the development of the West Asheville area of Buncombe County. On April 27, 1830, Robert's fourteen-year-old daughter, Mary Louise "Polly" Henry, married twenty-three-year-old Reuben Deaver, the son of Revolutionary War soldier William R. Deaver Jr. and Susannah Smith.

It seems probable that Deaver met his future bride during one of the Henry family visits to her grandfather's home in Waynesville. Since a boy of twelve, Reuben had been raised by Colonel Robert Love and was living there in 1830. It was said that Colonel Love liked Reuben as much as his own children.[120]

Reuben was already quite accomplished. In 1826–27, when barely out of his teens, he had served as a deputy surveyor during the division of Cherokee lands in Macon County, North Carolina. When the principal surveyors were unable to finish the plat maps, Reuben was pulled from the field and asked to do so. Although a short deadline loomed in front of him, he quickly completed the maps using the field notes. His maps are now housed in the state archives in Raleigh. A sign of his good moral character was his service as the corresponding secretary of the Haywood County Auxiliary of the American Bible Society in October 1830.[121]

In November 1830, Reuben traveled to Tennessee with his mentor and new grandfather-in-law Robert Love. The opportunity to settle the "Western Country" was attractive to many of the early Carolina pioneers. Thousands of acres of Revolutionary War bounty lands and ceded Indian lands were irresistible to restless settlers and greedy speculators. The Love family already owned large tracts of land in Tennessee. The journey's purpose, according to Deaver, was to view Madison County, Tennessee land that may become available to him due to a division of lands between Robert Love and Love's son Thomas. A portion of these divided lands would be a gift to Reuben and Polly, provided they removed to Tennessee. The proposal immediately appealed to Reuben, and on his return to North Carolina, he began making preparations to relocate west. Polly's father had other ideas, and so shortly thereafter, another interesting opportunity was put forth by Robert Henry for Reuben's consideration.

Henry often traveled far from home and was of the opinion that his plantation was not being managed well in his absence. It continued to be difficult for the farm to produce sufficient food and supplies for the Henry family and the slaves, and occasionally it became necessary to obtain supplementary provisions from outside sources. Corn, pork and bacon were often purchased from neighboring farmers.

Robert needed a solution. It seems he was either unable or unwilling to bring about the repair and upgrading required to adequately improve production. He even considered selling his slaves and giving up farming altogether. Perhaps he, too, was filled with wanderlust and saw only visions of a new life in the Western Country.

An attempt was made to sell the springs, but Robert Love suggested that something profitable might be done with them instead. The waters of the spring were already being taken into Asheville for the benefit of travelers visiting that city.[122] Love's idea sparked the imagination of Henry. A meeting was held that included Henry; his wife, Dorcas Bell; and Reuben Deaver.

Robert believed that son-in-law Deaver was an energetic, industrious young man, but poor, and he intended to help him. He proposed to Reuben that he could continue what he had started and bring the declining plantation back to life. He told Deaver he thought the springs would be a "big place" after a while, and if he (Deaver) would take that place and make improvements, it would be for him and his wife to keep. Deaver agreed to the generous and ambitious plan, and the dream of living in virgin Tennessee territory was abandoned by both parties. Henry had found a resolution to his management dilemma, and Deaver was assured a stable future.

Neither Robert nor his new partner was acquainted with making and keeping a place "for boarders who come from sickly to healthy sections of country for the sake of health." Nevertheless, they decided to move their families into Henry's home located at the foot of a hill, probably the new frame house built in 1828 or 1829, and start taking in boarders. The arrangement was designed as a test, the results of which would establish whether a profitable business could be supported.

> *On the 28th day of August 1830, the Cane Branch ceased to run. T. Moore's Creek and Ragsdale Creeks ceased to run some days before this. Corn died with drought. This has been the dryest summer in 60 years to my knowledge. Note our spring ceased to run some weeks previous to the above date.*

In the fall of 1831, after the Deaver family moved into Henry's home, Reuben again traveled to Tennessee, this time with Robert Henry. Their goal was to collect outstanding accounts owed to Henry, and any monies they recovered would help finance their new venture. The trip was partially successful, and Reuben returned in the spring of 1832. He joined the rest of his new family in the Henry home and began supervising plantation and business operations.

The Henry home soon began taking in boarders. With the funds collected in Tennessee and some cash advanced by Henry, Reuben opened a general store, stocking the shelves with merchandise and various goods to attract more guests.

Believing their experiment was proving successful, the entrepreneurs decided to build a new and larger boardinghouse. A location was selected on the top of a nearby hill about four hundred yards from the springs and close to the Bear Creek Road. The site offered a commanding view of the countryside and mountains in every direction. Alexander Henry, who had built Robert's first home, and his assistant, "black boy Jack," were enlisted as the contractors.

The "Corner House," as it came to be called, was built before June 1832 and was promoted to the public as "Deaver's Sulphur Springs." The two-story building stood forty-five feet by fifty-one feet, less fifteen feet square in the ell, and contained six rooms. Furniture, dishes and other supplies were borrowed from Deaver's new "Store House." Robert's wife and her daughters sewed bed sheets, curtains, quilts, tablecloths and towels to furnish rooms. Reuben's brother Joseph Deaver lived in the house and assisted in attending the store and with other business about the plantation.

Timber for construction of the Corner House was cut from trees on Henry's plantation, as well as from the neighboring farms of Moore, Poston, Case, Johnson and Hawkins. Logs were first processed into usable lumber at a mill located in the Bent Creek area and then hauled back to the Henry plantation using Deaver's oxen and Henry's horse team. Transporting wagonloads of timber to distant sawmills and returning with finished building lumber proved to be both expensive and difficult. During one of Reuben's trips to the mill, a valuable horse worth sixty dollars was killed. It was then evident to Henry that having a sawmill located on his own property was vital. In 1832, the North Carolina legislature authorized "Robert Henry to build a mill on Hominy Creek in Buncombe County."

Water power for mill operation was captured by building a wooden dam across Hominy Creek, an eastwardly running waterway that empties into the French Broad River. Hominy's course snaked around rolling hills, looping back and forth in several places. In those years, one of these loops formed the shape of a large horseshoe, with the open end facing north. The creek turned south at the northwestern corner of the horseshoe opening before curving eastward to form the bottom of the loop, and then back northward. The creek continued its northerly course to near the mouth of Caney Creek, where it again curved and returned to a northeastward flow. The timber

An old mill on Reems Creek near Weaverville, North Carolina. *North Carolina Collection, Pack Memorial Public Library, Asheville, NC.*

dam was constructed a short distance upstream from the northwest corner of the open loop.

The dam interrupted and partially diverted the original flow of Hominy Creek into a new man-made channel. Water flowing through this channel, or "race," would provide the water flow needed for their first sawmill.

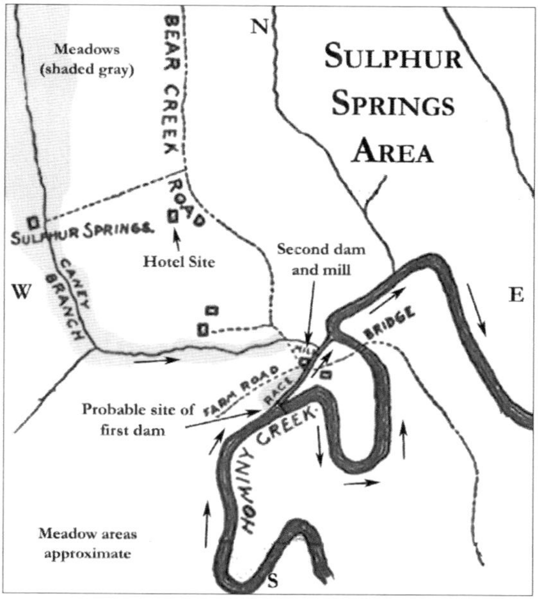

Portion of map from *Falls of Neuse Manufacturing Co. vs. Hendricks*, Supreme Court of North Carolina, May 18, 1890. Location of meadow, dam and hotel sites added by author.

James Williams, aided by Henry slaves Jack, Jim, Andy, Dub, Ben and a number of other hired hands, began digging the channel. Jack also assisted in framing and in hauling gravel above the dam spoiling and rock used between the mill sills. The race began at the dam and continued east to intersect the northeastern loop of the horseshoe near the mouth of Caney Creek. The race was approximately three hundred yards in length, eight feet wide and from six to eight feet deep, with a small portion about sixteen to twenty feet deep where it passed through a gap in the hill.

Undoubtedly, this must have been backbreaking and extremely difficult work. An impressive feat of strength was attributed to a fifteen-year-old slave named Jim. It was said that "in digging the mill race, [Jim] was able to throw clay out of the bottom of the race when it was eighteen feet deep with a shovel."

On the other hand, worker Abraham Fullbright felt Robert Henry's presence and physical contribution to the labor efforts were not of much consequence, noting, "Mr. Henry was along (in hauling the gravel and rock) and…in one of the trips, Mr. Henry took charge of the boat and sunk it, and we would not let him have charge of the boat anymore."

Construction of the dam on this site ultimately proved expensive and troublesome. Frequently breaking, the wooden structure often required repair. The creek bed underneath was principally rock, running from the southern side of the creek and continuing halfway across, where it changed to a sandy foundation. Fullbright recalled, "It always broke on the side where it was not a rock foundation near the head of the race. I do not know if it was underpinned at all."

Years later, a new dam and set of mills were built downstream. Remains of the replacement dam are still visible in the waters and on the banks of the race, about one hundred feet east of the Old Bear Creek Road bridge. What may be timber remnants of the earlier or original dam are visible in the water approximately three hundred feet west of the bridge.

By the end of the first summer, Henry and Deaver had netted a handsome profit of $200. The financial future of their enterprise appeared promising. At times, the boardinghouse was so full that overflow boarders were lodged in the Henry home.

On June 14, 1832, near the beginning of the lodging season, Robert Pinckney Deaver, son of Reuben and Polly, was born in the Corner House. With a new member of the family and positive cash flow, life was good for Reuben. He acquired land of his own, entering on January 20, 1833, for a state grant of 150 acres on Hominy Creek. By 1833, he was acting as postmaster of Sulphur Springs.

> [On] *Thursday 14th June 1832, Robert P. Deaver was born.*

The number of boarders at the springs was still increasing, and further improvements were planned, so it seemed prudent to enter into a more formal partnership agreement. At the conclusion of another successful summer season, Robert drafted a document titled "Articles of Agreement," which both parties enthusiastically signed on November 3, 1833.

Under the terms of the agreement, a sum of money would be advanced to Reuben and recorded in a book of entries. Reuben was to complete the set of mills on Hominy Creek, which were already under construction, with building expenses, excluding labor, paid equally. The expenses and profits of the operation belonged to Deaver, who would have the use of and profits from the mills until such profits reimbursed him for his expenses. Rights to the other improvements made and those later completed at the Sulphur Springs were to belong to Deaver.

Reuben agreed to supply Robert Henry's family in "victuals" and clothing except for Robert Henry's two sons, William L. and Robert M., and he would not be required to incur the cost of their schooling.

The agreement could be dissolved with twelve months' notice or on the death of either party. Upon dissolution, Deaver's improvements would remain his unless Henry agreed to pay their determined value. Deaver was to pay Henry the principal sum in the entries book, with a possible year or two indulgence in interest due. The mills would belong to Robert Henry as long as Deaver had been reimbursed for his expenses, excluding profits. If the profits had not reimbursed Deaver, the mills would go to Henry when the profits had reimbursed him. Henry's slaves, placed under the control of Deaver at the beginning of the agreement, would revert back to Henry.

With the security and protection of a legal document to safeguard him, Reuben proceeded full steam ahead. He had ambitious plans for development and expansion, and he began implementation. Over the next several years, he used all the profits he made at the store, over $2,200 received from Henry prior to and from their agreement, plus another $15,000 to complete his vision. In addition, he had the use of Henry's slaves and the labor of Henry's family.

The condition of the plantation was brought back, the land replenished and the fencing repaired to protect the crops. "He [Deaver] did a great deal of manuring on the old land. I helped to haul one spring 50 or 60 loads," said Abraham Fulbright.

The valley land adjoining Caney Creek was low and flat and became known as the "meadow." The meadow was about fifty yards wide at the narrowest point and ran from Bear Creek Road westward along the Caney Branch surrounding the springs and continuing to within sixty yards of the old Haywood Road. The meadow had been cleared and ditched previously by Henry, but portions were now becoming overgrown and turning back into swampy wetlands. Because of standing water, no grass could be cut. Elias Stines stated:

> *They cut down some wild grass the fall before in water ½ leg deep and carried it out on poles. The next spring, I cut the ditch. There was about half the meadow below he* [Deaver] *put in cultivation between 8 and 10 acres. He ditched above the spring and about it and put it in meadows. Deaver re-cleared the old meadow and cleared and ditched more acres.*

The original Corner House, now too small to accommodate the growing number of guests, was slated for major expansion. New wings were added, extending east and west with a covered walkway between them. The finished resort eventually included a bar room, dining room, parlor, cook kitchen and pantry, baking room and a servants' dining room with kitchen.

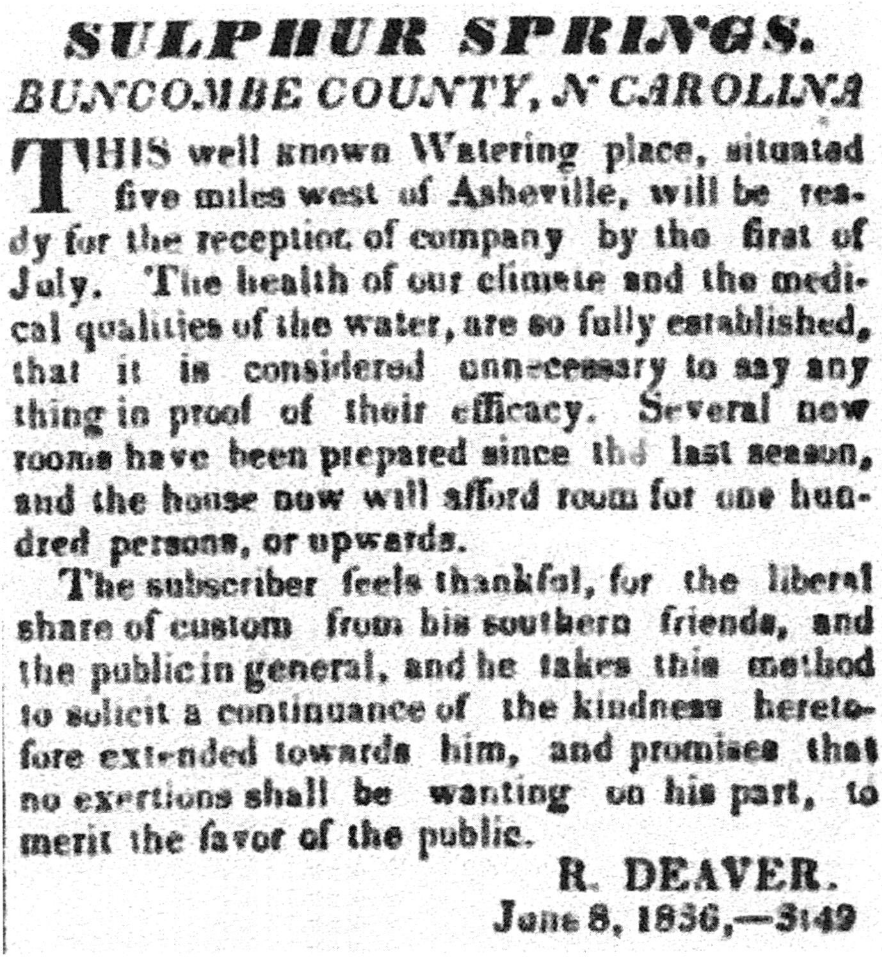

SULPHUR SPRINGS.
BUNCOMBE COUNTY, N CAROLINA

THIS well known Watering place, situated five miles west of Asheville, will be ready for the reception of company by the first of July. The health of our climate and the medical qualities of the water, are so fully established, that it is considered unnecessary to say any thing in proof of their efficacy. Several new rooms have been prepared since the last season, and the house now will afford room for one hundred persons, or upwards.

The subscriber feels thankful, for the liberal share of custom from his southern friends, and the public in general, and he takes this method to solicit a continuance of the kindness heretofore extended towards him, and promises that no exertions shall be wanting on his part, to merit the favor of the public.

R. DEAVER.
June 8, 1836,—3149

The June 25, 1836 issue of the *Carolina Watchman*. *North Carolina Collection, Pack Memorial Public Library, Asheville, NC.*

Over time, a barn, cribs for grain storage, a machine shop, a well and well house, a smith shop, a poultry house, a smokehouse and a threshing machine were added. A gristmill was built down at the creek in 1840. Additional outbuildings were built for the comfort and enjoyment of visitors and boarders, including log cabins—the "lower cabins" near the spring, upper cabins and a family cabin with kitchen. These cabins included brick chimneys. Slave cabins were also built, less comfortable and commodious than those for the guests, with chimneys constructed of rock, wood and clay.

A one-hundred-foot by twenty-five-foot horse stable was built, as well as a carriage shelter with an open stable. Slave Sam served as the ostler, meeting and greeting weary travelers and those seeking cool breezes and healthy waters and caring for their horses.

A Spring House was constructed down the hill from the hotel complex at the Sulphur Springs, which included a bathhouse outfitted with two copper boilers, five partitions with bathing tubs, a water wheel and a reservoir.

I put the Rock Basin in the Sulphur Spring [on] *the 16th* [of] *June 1834.*

In the spring of 1834, one of Robert's contributions was the installation of a rock basin to control the flow of water. Water was directed from an aperture in the bottom of the basin to a cistern within a small building. A wire-and-pulley system filled buckets with cistern water and transported them up the hill to the hotel, where a waterman was on duty at all times. The waters became famous for their medicinal and healing properties and were said to be excellent for dyspepsia and increasing the appetite.

Three privies were added—two with pits, and one without. Decorative gardens were planted, and new orchards near the tavern house supplemented one growing at the old house.

> *From the back of the kitchen to the first stake is Brown apples, from the first to the second stake is Sweet apples, from the 2nd to the 3rd stake is Queen apples from Wilkes, from the 3rd to the 4th are Vandivers from Stevilys* [of] *Burke, from the 4th to the end of the row are Limbir Twiggs. Then from the beginning at the dairy to the first stake are Limbir Twiggs, then from the first to the 2nd are Rose apples, from the 2nd to the 3rd English Pairmains, from the 3rd to the 4th are Winter Cheese apples, then to the end are Brevard apples. Lower garden from the creek to the first stake are Horse Apples, from the first to the 2nd are Beeff Apples.*[123]

In addition, "there were bowling alleys, billiard tables, shuffle-boards and other games. A large ball-room and a string band, composed of free negroes from Charleston and Columbia, provided the music for dancing," and Deaver brought in a Frenchman named Coche as a confectionery and pastry cook.[124]

At a cost of about $150 to $200, Reuben built a new road to the Sulphur Springs. Running from the old road on the top of the hill near Mr. Tate's, the road was a mile and a half to a mile and three quarters in length and

Believed to be an early sketch of the mountains located southwest of the hotel. *Henry Archive (private collection).*

included a bridge over the branch near the springs. It continued from there, intersecting the old road beyond the springs.

While Deaver oversaw and directed most of the work and improvements as per their agreement, Robert Henry used the power of his name, money and influence to benefit the advancement of the Sulphur Springs and surrounding community. Although he may not have excelled at rowing a boat and was perhaps too advanced in age to help with manual labor, he contributed in his own manner.

A portion of the original 770 acres located on a hill above and west of the springs was set aside by Henry for use as a cemetery. Originally nine acres, it is now a small section of three acres surrounded by the property of Asheville School and still in use today. According to Robert, the first person buried there was South Carolina resident John Kitt [Keitt], in 1836. Keitt's name appears in the first Sulphur Springs hotel register. Several members of the Henry family, including Dorcas Bell Henry and William L. Henry, are entombed in the cemetery, as are Reuben Deaver and other members of the Deaver family. The cemetery includes a slave section in the rear, with many unmarked grave sites and others identifiable only by fieldstones.

Much of Robert Henry's original land in West Asheville is now the Malvern Hills subdivision. *Author's collection.*

Graves of Dorcas B. Henry, Reuben Deaver and members of the William L. Henry family at the Sulphur Springs Cemetery. *Author's collection.*

> *John Kitt* [Keitt] *of So. Carolina died & was buried on the 27th August 1836 & was the first that was buried at the Sulphur Springs Meeting House.*

Robert had served as the first teacher in Buncombe County, and now he would establish his own school for the community. The first location may have been in the Henry home, as T.J. Walter states he taught school at Sulphur Springs in 1832, earning three dollars per quarter as tuition. Teachers named Bryant and Miss Bradshaw also taught at the school. Class size was usually from ten to fifteen scholars per session.

On April 21, 1835, Robert deeded seven acres of his John Jarrett land to be used for the "Sulphur Springs Academy" in "consideration of the desire of the improvement of youth." Trustees of the academy were Charles Moore, John Hawkins, George W. Jones, G.W. Candler and Reuben Deaver.

In 1836, Robert, at his own expense, erected the Sulphur Springs Meeting House, or Academy, to function as a church and school. The meetinghouse was located immediately in front of the graveyard. The first session appears to have been taught by G.A. Mathis in March 1836. Other teachers included E. Tate in 1839–40, William Hawkins from 1838 to 1845 or later and M. Smith in 1840. Children from the Riley, Cannon, Jones, Hawkins and Moore families were among those who studied at the academy.

The meetinghouse was a regular stop for Baptist and Methodist circuit-riding preachers well into the 1860s. Services were held for both whites and slaves, sometimes jointly. Reverend John Reynolds gave sermons the

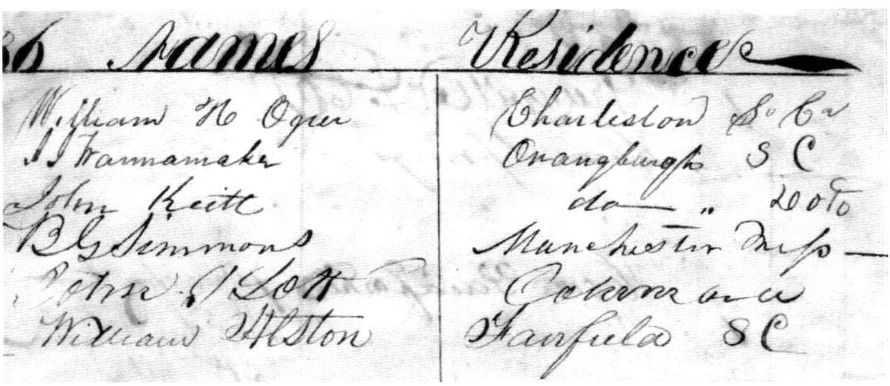

The Sulphur Springs Hotel register from 1836. Note John Keitt as a registered guest. *North Carolina Collection, Pack Memorial Public Library, Asheville, NC.*

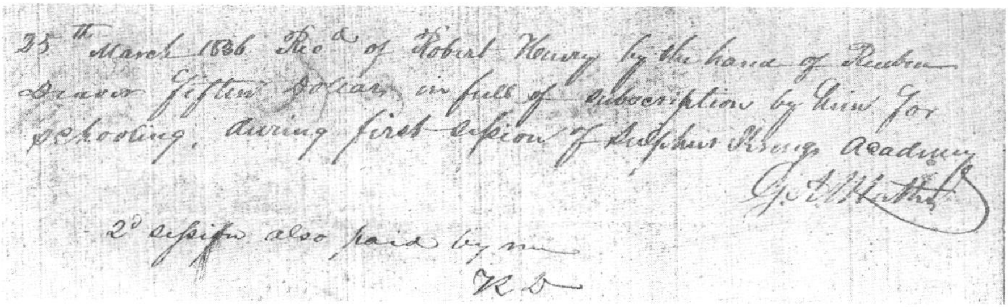
25th March 1836 Rec'd of Robert Henry by the hand of Reuben Deaver Fifteen Dollars in full of subscription by him for schooling during first session of Sulphur Spring Academy

2d session also paid by me
R. D.

The first school session at the Sulphur Springs Academy was held in 1836. *North Carolina Department of Archives and History.*

first Sunday of each month. Names of others known to have preached there over the years include Byrd; Smith; Dr. Cummings; Mr. Moody, a Baptist; McMahan, Reverend Baldwin; Tom Glenn; and Miller.[125]

There seemed to be no end to Henry and Deaver's success. Benefiting from newspaper advertising and great press reviews, the resort became very well known, especially by those living in South Carolina. It was noted, "The position of these Springs make them a delightful summer resort. There is always a pleasant, cool breeze stirring. The view, from almost any point of the grounds, is fine, presenting, in front, the Blue Ridge and its spurs; in the west, Mount Pisgah; and the Haywood Mountains."[126]

One reviewer commented on the "cool constant breezes which make existence a luxury. To these add mountain butter; crystal, snowy honey, fat mutton; large orchard of luscious apples for the children and young folks; a bowling alley and shuffle-board for the active; and white sulphur water for all who need it, and you have in these the charms which conjure back the roses to the pale cheek."[127] Another claimed, "Sulphur Springs is superior in both natural beauty and in the society gathered there to the better known Saratoga Springs in New York."[128]

An 1837 description stated, "The House is built on a high hill between two branches about 200 yards from each...in the form of an L, one side about 150 feet long, the other 120; two stor[ies] with piazzas running all around out-side to each story; upstairs is divided into 29 or 30 lodging rooms."[129] The hotel was able to accommodate over one hundred lodgers. Weekly board was five dollars per week, or four dollars per week for an extended stay. One could board his horse for an additional two dollars per week.[130]

The spring's waters were said to benefit the skin and kidneys and act as a tonic. Maximum therapeutic dose was one gallon per day, with a minimum of one half gallon. It was used internally to treat dyspepsia and externally as a bath for skin disorders.

A July 11, 1839 advertisement in the *Charleston Courier* boasted more rooms had been added since the previous season, and a warm bath would be in operation by the July 20. In 1837, Deaver had expressed his intention to construct a "commodious bathing house" with separate compartments whereby one could enjoy either a cold or warm bath. The bathhouse was now completed.

Roads were "mostly cow trails going up the steepest part of a hill, following the crest as long as there was any level ground, and down again the steepest part."[131] An 1847 advertisement in the same newspaper noted the road to the springs from the hotel was now greatly improved and that a daily hack running between there and Asheville was available. A post office was on the premises. For boarders with children, "Mr. Gamewell, a

Sulphur Springs historic marker on Smoky Park Highway, West Asheville. *Photo by author.*

member of the Junior Class of Columbia College, S.C., will open a school at the Sulphur Springs about 1st of July and continue it through the watering season. Mr. Gamewell comes highly recommended as possessing the highest qualifications as a teacher. Board for students may be had at the Hotel, or in respectable private residences at moderate rates."

A large ballroom was attached to the building.[132] For entertainment and music, J. Randle's [Randall] band was engaged for the season. Randall is said to have been a free Negro from South Carolina who had been presented with $5,000 for giving information about a slave insurrection in Charleston. Another musician by the name of Lapitude owned a plantation near Charleston with forty slaves.[133]

By 1848, the resort was "village-like, with a little cluster of buildings which could accommodate two hundred guests and their accompanying servants and horses."[134] The *Carolina Watchman* reported in April 8, 1849, that the hotel had "647 boarders last season, mostly from South Carolina, also 55 children, 153 servants and 375 horses." Peak season lasted approximately six weeks in the summer. Guests began arriving in June, but the largest crowds appeared about the third week of July. During the first week of September, guests began leaving to return home.

An extensive description was given in November 1849 by Mr. A. McKeithen in a letter written to his cousin:

> *Col. Deaver is the proprietor and quite a gentleman. He is prepared for entertaining about 150 persons at a time. His building is in the form of an L, each wing 300 feet or more in length with double piazzas in front, or one for each story, and single piazza in the rear, with a large dining room and kitchen attached nearly at one end, forming three sides of a hollow square. I do not know how many fire rooms belong to the building, as I have not inquired nor counted the chimneys. Considerable fixings anyway.*
>
> *The spring is 400 yards from the house in a valley, rises perpendicular through the mud which is about 3 feet deep and through sand and gravel underneath. It reminds me of a quagmire…gives way or shakes when you step on it.*
>
> *The proprietor has a granite basin with a small hole in the centre of the bottom inserted into the mud and sand through which the water rises. I do not know the perpendicular height of the rock in the upper end of which the basin is made. The basin will contain 15 gallons and when bailed dry will be filled in 15 minutes. There is a small gap on the upper edge of the basin*

SULPHUR

SPRINGS,

Buncombe county, N. C.

THE Proprietor of the Sulphur SPRINGS, in Buncombe county, North Carolina, four and a half miles west of Asheville, begs leave to inform his old visitors, and the public generally, that his entire establishment is in excellent repair, and open to accommodate from one hundred and fifty, to two hundred persons. His buildings have been lately enlarged—his stables thorougly refitted—his bath houses and pleasure grounds well prepared, and from his success heretofore, he hopes to continue to riceive a liberal share of public patronage.

He would, also, respectfully inform southern gentlemen, who may desire summer residences in the mountain country, that he has a number of beautiful sites in the vicinity of the springs, which he will dispose of on the most reasonable terms.

N. B. Timber and every advantage for building at hand.

R. DEAVER, *Proprietor.*

July, 1840. bt—8

Highland Messenger, July 1840, Asheville, North Carolina. *North Carolina Collection, Pack Memorial Public Library, Asheville, NC.*

and a conductor attached to convey the water into a small house near the spring in which there is a cistern or trough kept full, from which posts are put into the ground some 12 or more feet apart all the way to the house in a direct line. To these posts are attached arms with upright irons to which a large wire is fixed, and rollers under the wire. On this wire, a bucket is sent

> *off from the house with a cord fastened to it. The cord runs on the rollers, the bucket goes into this cistern or trough, is filled and brought to the house by this cord. The waterman is at the house all the time. I have said enough about the spring, only the taste of the water as its farewell, as it is called is exactly like the scent of a rotten egg (not the worst). No company here now, the season for that being over.*[135]

Frederick Law Olmsted visited the mountains in July 1854. In his observations of Sulphur Springs, he described

> *a white, wooden building with a long piazza for smokers, loungers, and flirters, and a bowling alley and shuffle board; with coaches and trotting wagons at the stable; poor women picking blackberries, poor men bringing fowls, school girls studiously climbing romantic rocks and otherwise making themselves as pretty as possible, children fighting their black nurses, and old gold spectacles stopping me to inquire if I was the mail and if I had not got a newspaper.*[136]

But disaster struck in March 1861. Late at night on the thirteenth or early on the fourteenth, the Henry family was suddenly awakened. C.C. Henry recalled, "Uncle Andy woke us in the night by hollering, 'What a fire!' Yes, the hotel was burned this night & set afire."[137] The hotel "was fired in several places and no doubt was the work of an incendiary," and there was "not a cent of insurance."[138] The hotel building, all the furniture and several out buildings were casualties of the arson. The loss was estimated at $12,000. Robert's daughter-in-law, Cornelia Henry, grieved. "It will be a long time if ever we get over the loss," she wrote. "I hope the guilty persons will yet be found & suffer the penalty. If justice never overtakes them in the world, it will certainly in the next." Her husband, William, was now "prematurely an old man." Robert Henry must have been as devastated when he heard the news. His and Reuben Deaver's crown jewel was gone forever.

The perpetrators remain unknown, although Cornelia had her suspicions, stating "Oh! How I would love to see one woman hung, but I must bear in mind that 'Vengeance is mine I will repay,' said the Lord." Still bitter over their loss, in the midst of the Civil War, she gives the name of an employee living in a cabin near the hotel. "F.M. Corn took dinner here. I can't bear Corn, for I believe he had a hand in the burning of the hotel. He is mean enough for anything, I think." She also complained that Corn had "gone to the Yankees."

Corn had been employed to repair the hotel and worked sheep for a man named C.C. Terry, who was contracted to manage the hotel in 1860. Terry had previously managed the Mountain House.[139] In 1861, when Terry's management term at Sulphur Springs was completed, William Henry wanted him out, but Terry and his family refused to leave. Henry and Terry chose to have the matter settled by arbitration, but it did not go well for Henry. On February 27, Henry went to Asheville for the arbitrator's decision. "Terry gets the house this year for $500 and allows Mr. Henry nothing for last year. Oh! He is a vile old wretch as ever went unhung," wrote Cornelia Henry.

There was certainly bad blood between the Henry and Terry families. During one particular instance, C.C. Henry recalled:

> *At night, Jim Nichols & a man named Cole came down about 11 o'clock (two patrols) saying* [slave] *George was at the stillhouse playing the fiddle for them to dance, which so provoked Mr.* [William] *Henry, as he had given him a pass to his wife's house telling him not to stop at the stillhouse. But the men deceived him & had the negro to come & play for them.* [The] *Terrys (the old man & two boys) picked a fuss with Mr. Henry, and they had a general row. Mr. Henry & negro George come out with no bones broken, 'tho George got a lick on the neck which will disable him several days. Old Terry got a hole through one ear besides other scratches & so ended that row. I fear they will have more of it yet.*[140]

On Thursday, February 28, William went to Bent Creek to obtain a warrant for Terry and his boys. He returned with Tom Hendrix, who had also gone to get a warrant, as the Terrys had threatened his life. Less than three weeks later, the hotel was burned to the ground.

The site lay in ruins until 1887, when a larger, three-story brick hotel opened in the same location, built by lumber baron Edwin G. Carrier. Known first as the Sulphur Springs Hotel, it was renamed Carrier's Springs and then the Belmont. A new wing was added in the winter of 1890. Carrier constructed the area's first hydroelectric plant on Hominy Creek, which powered lights and a passenger elevator. In 1893, he built a steel bridge over the French Broad River and ran rails for an electric trolley line between Asheville and the Belmont.[141] The hotel was later converted into a sanitarium, leased in 1891 by Dr. Karl von Ruck. An 1892 advertisement boasted steam heat, grate-fired private baths, an electric elevator and gas lights. The Belmont Hotel was destroyed by fire in August 1892.

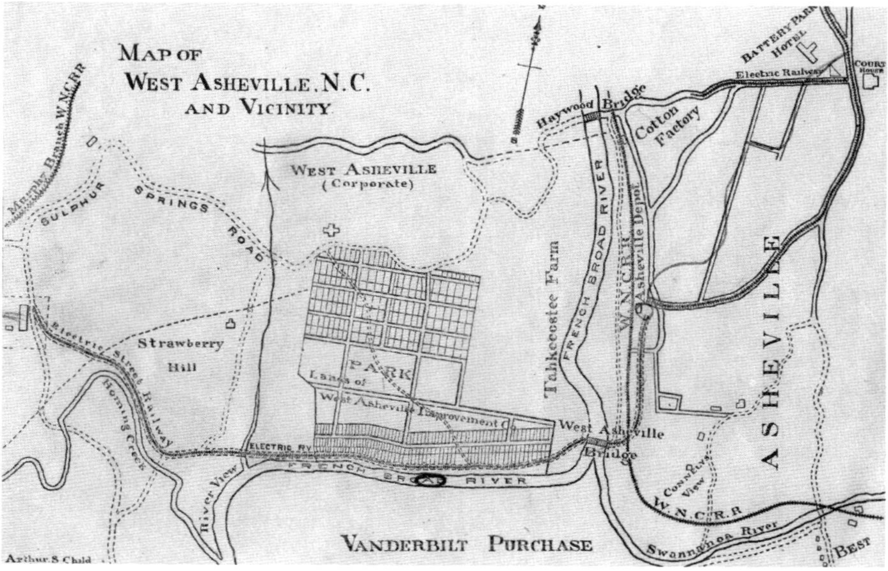

The Belmont Hotel (extreme left) featured the addition of an electric street railway to Asheville. From the West Asheville Improvement Company booklet, 1890. *North Carolina Collection, Pack Memorial Public Library, Asheville, NC.*

Remains of the Belmont Hotel in 1903. *North Carolina Collection, Pack Memorial Public Library, Asheville, NC.*

Top: Carrier's Sulphur Springs Hotel prior to 1890 wing addition. *Middle*: Hotel Belmont (renamed). *North Carolina Collection, Pack Memorial Public Library, Asheville, NC. Bottom*: The Belmont Hotel after an 1890 wing addition. *From* Souvenir of Asheville or the Sky-Land *(1892), by Mrs. Harriet Adams Sawyer.*

Right: Edwin G. Carrier built a large hotel on the site of Henry and Deaver's Sulphur Springs resort and constructed the first hydroelectric plant on Hominy Creek. *North Carolina Collection, Pack Memorial Public Library, Asheville, NC.*

Below: Otto Schoenfeld and family during a 1907 visit to Asheville. The pavilion is believed to be located at Sulphur Springs, which Schoenfeld had recently purchased. *Courtesy of the family of Otto B. Schoenfeld.*

The Malvern Hills Country Club, circa 1926. *North Carolina Collection, Pack Memorial Public Library, Asheville, NC.*

Remains of the early twentieth-century octagon that covered the Sulphur Spring. *Author's collection.*

Left: Support structures for one of the Henry mills may be seen on the bank of the race. *Courtesy of Vance Pollock.*

Right: A plaque honoring Robert Henry and slave Sam was displayed at the Malvern Hills Country Club. *Courtesy of Bill Rhodes.*

Due to the loss of the hotel, his orange groves in Florida suffering a severe freeze and other problems, Carrier was forced out of the hotel business and went back to timbering. Eventually, the Asheville Electric Company became owner of the property and on November 6, 1906, sold the Sulphur Springs Farm and the Spring Tract, a total of 59.8 acres, to Otto B. Schoenfeld of New Orleans for $30,500. Schoenfeld, who had won the world title in fencing at the Paris Exposition in 1900 and was the first American to have competed in Olympic fencing, envisioned that a "health farm" would be built there.

It was probably Schoenfeld who built a new concrete pavilion over the spring, replacing an older wooden structure. In 1913, he sold the same tract to a friend, Lawrence Fabacher, also of New Orleans. Then, in 1914, Fabacher sold the property to the Sulphur Springs Park Realty Company, of which Schoenfeld was a vice-president. Plans for a resort hotel on the same site as previous ventures and a large subdivision were designed but never built.

Much of the Henry plantation and Sulphur Springs land is now a West Asheville subdivision built by another developer. The Malvern Hills Country Club stood on the site of the springs in the 1920s, incorporating Schoenfeld's octagonal structure that had encompassed the spring outlet. A nine-hole golf course lay within the Meadow along Caney Branch.

Little evidence exists of the once-famous Sulphur Springs, but one may still see a few vine-covered tubs, mounds of bricks and the vestiges of the twentieth-century octagon. The meadow remains as a sparsely wooded valley and lowland area around Caney Creek. The mill sites on Hominy Creek and the race have nearly vanished.

Chapter 10

Transitions

At Hill's old place on Cumberland Mountain on the night of 12 of Nov 1833, the stars shot & fell about as fast as a moderate shower of snow.

After signing the 1833 agreement with Deaver, Robert Henry wasted little time pursuing other interests. In less than two weeks, he was in the Cumberland Mountains of Tennessee. He wished to sell land and make collections on some he had previously sold. Stopping for the evening at a stagecoach way station and travelers' stand located on Hill's Trace, he witnessed a once-in-a-lifetime event. On the night of November 12, 1833, the Leonid meteor storm put on a phenomenal celestial display. It was said that "a tempest of falling stars broke over the Earth. North America bore the brunt of its pelting" and that "the sky was scored in every direction with shining tracks and illuminated with majestic fireballs." Witnesses stated, "The frequency of meteors was estimated to be about half that of flakes of snow in an average snowstorm. Their numbers were quite beyond counting."[142] It must have been a sight to behold.

In the days following the nighttime spectacle, Robert continued his westward journey. He found success in selling some land holdings and collected payment for several hundred acres near the Elk River in Lincoln County and near Mount Pinson.

Upon his return home to the springs, Robert began living more leisurely. He "remained as a boarder, continuous doing little business, other times reading history, travels and newspapers." Son-in-law Deaver was overseeing

A spectacular Leonid meteor storm occurred on the night of November 12–13, 1833. Image from a nineteenth-century woodcut. *General Conference Archives of the Seventh-day Adventists.*

the Sulphur Springs, so at age sixty-six, it was time for Robert to settle down and reap the rewards of years of hard work.

> *On the night of the 20th of May 1834, I heard the first South Carolina Whiper-will that I ever heard in Buncombe.*

But unexpected changes, disruptions and complications were coming, and Robert's new style of living would be short-lived. On May 14, 1835, Robert's daughter Eliza was wed to William G. Tidwell, a man Robert considered in possession of low character.

James Love Henry, the last child of Robert and Dorcas Bell, was born on December 24, 1835.[143] But by 1836, Robert's marriage of twenty-two years was falling apart. The couple had been disagreeing for years, according to Deaver. Dorcas Bell Love was only seventeen when she married Robert, a man thirty years her senior, and now Robert was nearly seventy, while she was just thirty-nine. Robert's drinking habit was affecting his marriage. He had partaken of whiskey as early as his Cowan's Ford experience, and probably earlier. Frequently helping himself to the spirits at the store and bar, he spent much time socializing with his friends. Employees noticed that he became "light" while working around the plantation. Neighbor Mary Gudger Moore related this anecdote regarding Robert's protection of his alcohol supply:

> *This old gentleman was also very fond of "bitters" and usually kept a bottle pretty well filled on the mantle in his room. On one occasion when he was a little indisposed, his negroes—and he had a yard full—being very attentive, coming in every morning to pay their respects to Old Master and inquire after his health. He noticed, as their visits became more frequent, his bitters went down. He waited till his bottle was quite low and poured a quantity of epicac and watched the results.*
>
> *In the morning, they came in as usual, and he observed that his bottle was pretty well drained. In a short time, he heard a terrible racket in the yard. Some little negroes came running in—"Everybody is sick. Would Old Master come out and see what was the matter?" He went and found them scattered all over the yard, down on their hands and knees vomiting for all they were worth. "Why, what's the matter?" said he. "Have you been eating or drinking to make you sick?" They admitted instantly that they had taken a little, just a sup, out of his bottle on the mantle. "Well, said he, you are all dumb niggers. That was poison I had mixed up to kill the rats." There was weeping and wailing*

and praying then. When the old gentleman had enjoyed the joke long enough, he said, "Well, as you have all vomited pretty well, perhaps you have thrown it up. I will have a large kettle of tea made from bitter herbs, and you must all drink about a gallon apiece and maybe you will get well." They did so and recovered, but he never had his bitters troubled any more.

Robert became abusive and jealous when drinking, Dorcas said, using "the most gross and inhuman language" and "frequently threatened her life."[144] Convinced that she was unfaithful, he often claimed son Robert M. Henry was not his own. Dorcas tolerated Robert's behavior "for the sake of her children" until June 11, 1836, when it "became the most cruel and barbarous." It was on that day that Robert ordered her to leave and threatened that if she did not, he would use force. Dorcas found "her life in danger and her condition intolerable," so she "prevailed on her parents to remove her to the paternal roof once more." Taking her daughter Martha and new baby, James, she fled to Waynesville to live with her father, Robert Love.

On the 11th day of June 1836, Dorcas B. Henry & [word erased] *parted from me & went to Haywood for good, not to return.*

Robert's "retirement" didn't last long either. Another opportunity with his son-in-law presented itself. The United States was preparing for the removal of the Cherokee from their tribal homelands, and western North Carolina was to be opened for white settlement. Under the terms of the 1835 Treaty of New Echota, the government initiated a process whereby the Cherokee, within two years, would be forced to relocate to Indian Territory west of the Mississippi River. This removal is now known as the Trail of Tears.

Before the land could be auctioned and sold to settlers or speculators, it had to be evaluated, surveyed and categorized. The surveyors were also instructed to record gold, lead, marble and other natural resources that were said to be abundant.[145]

Reuben Deaver saw a golden opportunity. In 1826 and 1827, he had been appointed as a deputy surveyor of Cherokee land in Macon County, and in April 1836, the Haywood County court authorized him to map its new Cherokee lands.[146] He felt he could benefit from this previous experience. In a shrewd and calculated move, probably anticipating the outcome of the November elections, Reuben sent a letter to gubernatorial candidate E.B. Dudley, who later became North Carolina's first governor chosen by popular vote. In the letter, Reuben requested appointment as principal surveyor of the newest lands ceded to the United States.

Mr. Dudley could do "without reading a long complimentary letter," Reuben wrote, "so I will venture to come to the point plainly at once: I suppose the legislature will provide for the surveying of the Cherokee lands lately acquired by Treaty. Now sir, to tell you the plain truth, I wish to be appointed the Principal Surveyor." He continued, "I will merely say that I am well acquainted with this mountainous country, and I do think that the appointment of me would give general satisfaction in the western counties."[147]

Reuben's directness and experience were convincing, and in 1837, he was appointed. Assistants on his surveys were John Sudderth, James Whitaker, James Gudger, Samuel Gudger, J.W. Hawkins, W.W. Piercy, G.F. Caler and his father-in-law, Robert Henry. At times, Robert's sons William L. and Robert M. served as chain bearers.[148]

It is no surprise that Robert would be (and would want to be) part of the survey teams. He was family, and his experience as a surveyor was well known. How could he be excluded? His wife had left him, the hotel was out of his control and he could have the independence he had always known and a lifestyle compatible with his manner of dress and love of the outdoors. He had seen the rivers and streams of the beautiful western North Carolina mountains before, and now he would have an advanced viewing of prime real estate. What did he have to lose?

In fact, Robert may have already been in and have taken a liking to the Cherokee land a year before the surveys. Eliza's husband, William G. Tidwell, had been in western North Carolina since October 1836 assisting as a chain bearer. He was accompanied by Robert's thirteen-year-old son, William. On October 5, Robert left home, traveling to Tidwell's for William, arriving there on the tenth. At one point, Robert had sent his slave Malinda to join them. Another slave, "Negro Jack," who Deaver had "learnt to be a carpenter," was sent because Robert "needed a better house."

Henry, Deaver and the survey teams found a beautiful country upon their arrival in the western North Carolina mountains. There was "evidences of ancient occupation, trails, burial grounds and mounds that bore the wrinkle of antiquity." The trails were often worn so bad by travel and weather that "a man could pass through them and not be seen in the steepest places; while in the hollow beyond, the soil had been washed and beaten down till the trail was a foot or two above the ground around it."[149]

The surveyors established 1,400 distinct tracts, ranging from fifty to four hundred acres. Deaver produced a detailed map illustrating the boundaries,

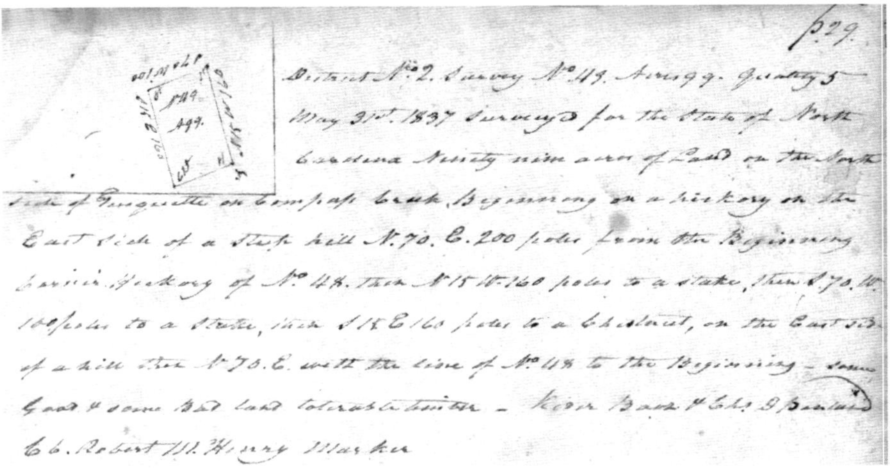

p.29

District No. 2. Survey No. 49. Acres 99. Quality 5
May 31st. 1837 Surveyed for the State of North
Carolina Ninety nine acres of Land on the North
side of Tusquittee on Compass Creek. Beginning on a hickory on the
East side of a steep hill N. 70. E. 200 poles from the Beginning
corner Hickory of No. 48. Then N 15 W. 160 poles to a stake, then S 70. W.
100 poles to a stake, then S 15 E 160 poles to a Chestnut, on the East side
of a hill then N 70. E. with the line of No. 48 to the Beginning – some
Good & some Bad land tolerable timber – Kiser Bark & Chs. G. Barlow
CC. Robert M. Henry Marker

Compass Creek survey plot and description from Robert Henry's survey notebook. *Courtesy of Don Taylor.*

Compass Creek is a tributary of Tusquittee Creek in Clay County, North Carolina. *Photo by author.*

mountains, rivers and creeks, with each property being ranked in value.[150] Any land worth twenty-five cents or more per acre was surveyed and then divided into five sections, depending on its determined value. First-class land was valued at no less than four dollars per acre, second-class no less than two dollars, third-class one dollar, fourth-class fifty cents and fifth-class no less than twenty-five cents per acre.[151]

Near the end of May 1837, Robert's survey team was running boundary lines in the area of Tusquittee Creek, near present-day Hayesville. Robert was crossing a small creek flowing down the mountain into the Tusquittee when he dropped his compass into the cold, rushing waters. He adopted the moniker "Compass Creek" for the tributary and entered it on his survey plat. The name continues to this day.[152]

Although various Buncombe County court records dated April 1838 and Fall 1839 state that Robert was a county resident, sometime between the surveys of 1837 and 1838, Robert made "The Nation" his permanent home and prepared to begin life as a farmer.[153]

In anticipation of the Cherokee removal, the United States constructed several forts to hold detainees. Fort Hembree, located on the south bank of the Hiwassee River about a mile southwest of Hayesville, was established in early October 1837. This army post served as the gathering point for Cherokees taken from the villages of Tusquittee, Shooting Creek and other nearby communities.[154]

President Martin Van Buren ordered General Winfield Scott to coordinate the removal, and beginning in late May, Scott began the forced evacuation into the forts. Among the 740 participating North Carolina Volunteers was Robert M. Henry, son of Robert. He assisted in gathering the Cherokee for three or four

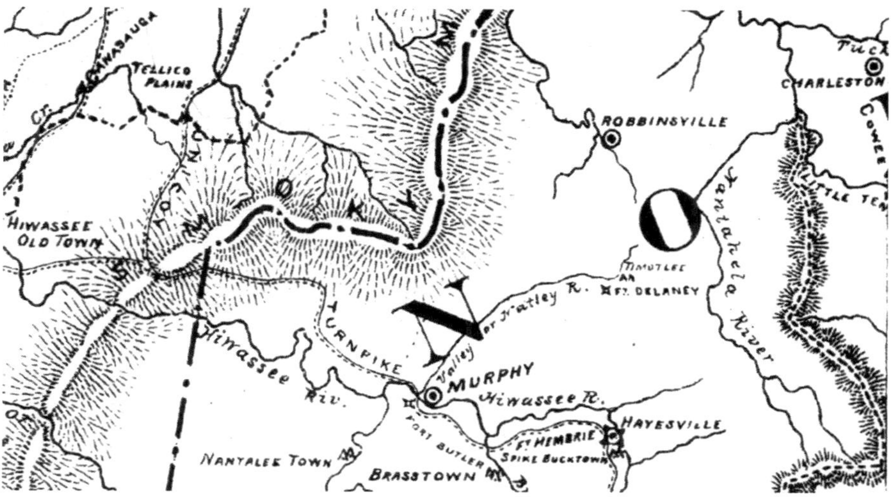

In 1838, Cherokee were gathered and held at Fort Hembree before being moved west. Portion of Map of the Former Territory of the Cherokee Nation of Indians, C. C. Royce, 1884. *North Carolina Collection, Pack Memorial Public Library, Asheville, NC.*

Right: A sketch of what is believed to be a Cherokee woman and child during the Indian Removal. From a sketchbook found among Robert Henry's papers and possibly belonging to G.F. Babbage. *Henry Archive (private collection).*

Below: When Robert Henry's brother John died, the remaining siblings—Joseph, Isaac and Rachel—gave slaves George and Andy to Robert. *North Carolina Collection, Pack Memorial Public Library, Asheville, NC.*

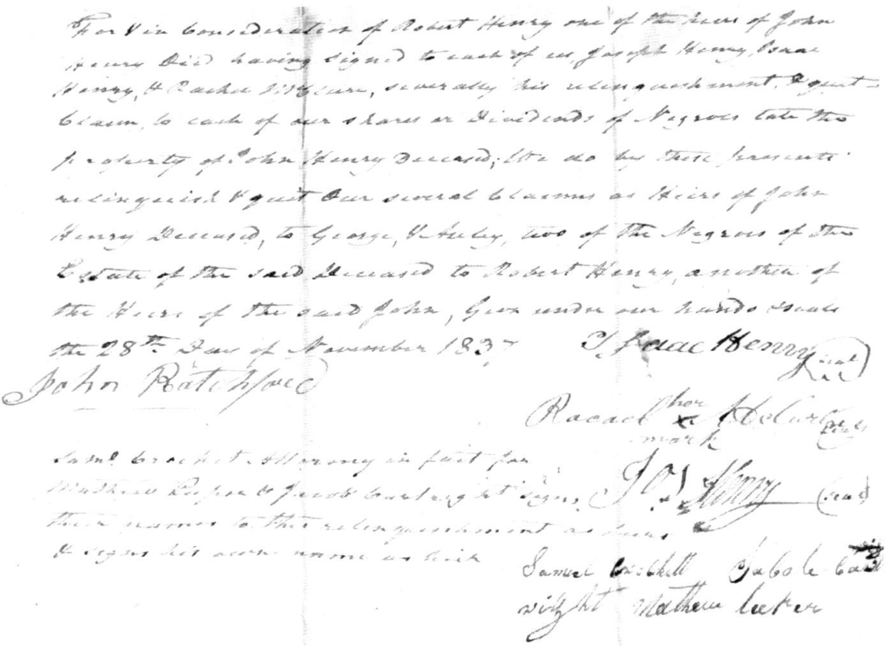

For & in consideration of Robert Henry one of the heirs of John Henry Decd having signed to each of us, Joseph Henry, Isaac Henry, & Rachel [illegible], severally his relinquishment & quit claim, to each of our shares or Dividends of Negroes late the property of John Henry Deceased; We do by these presents relinquish & quit Our several claims as Heirs of John Henry Deceased, to George, & Andy, two of the Negroes of the Estate of the said Deceased to Robert Henry, another of the Heirs of the said John, Given under our hands & seals the 28th Day of November 1837

Isaac Henry (seal)

John [illegible]

Racael her x [illegible] mark (seal)

Jos Henry (seal)

[illegible]

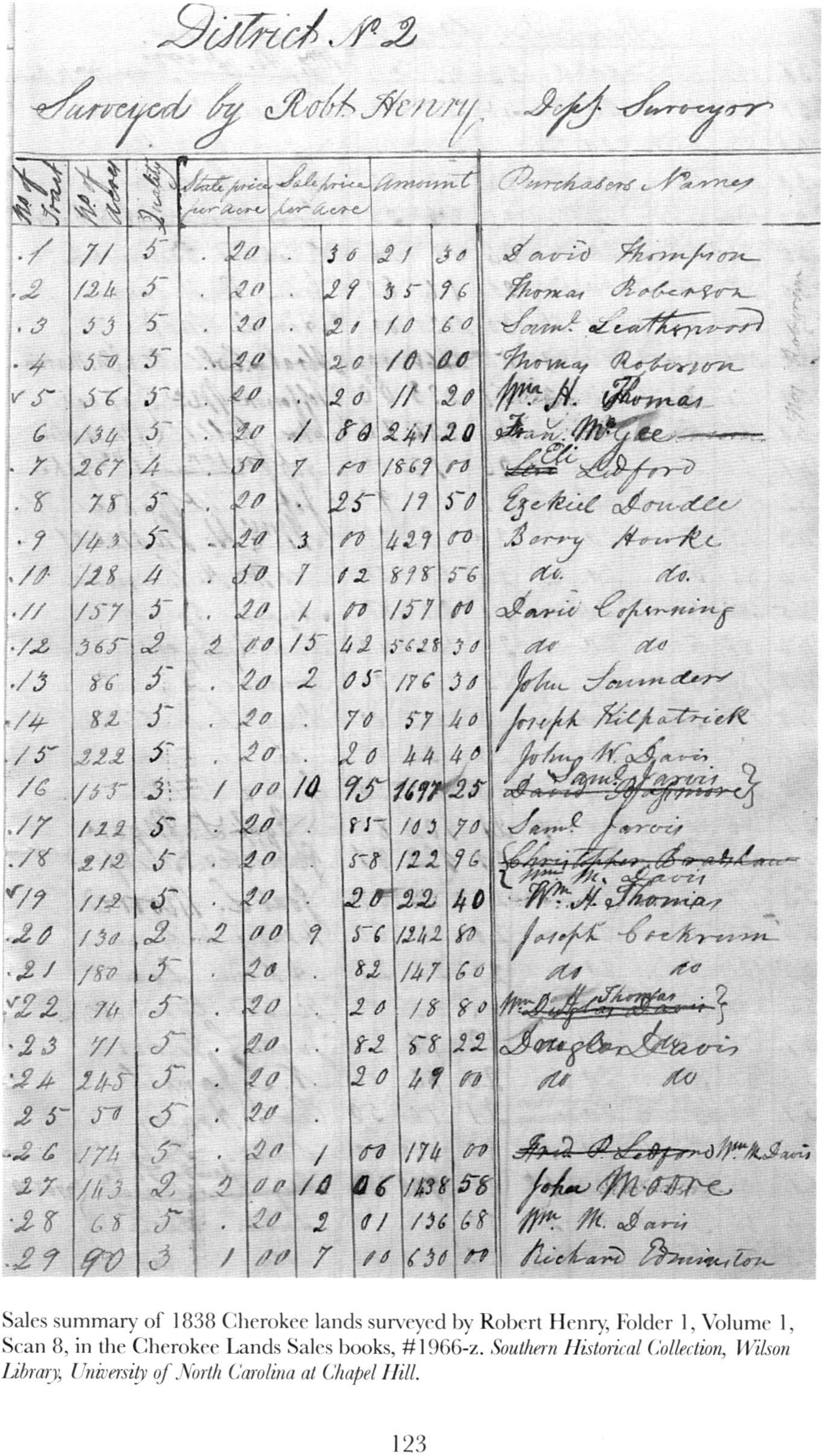

District No 2

Surveyed by Robt. Henry Depy. Surveyor

No. of Tract	No. of Acres	Quality	State price per acre		Sale price per acre		Amount		Purchasers Names
1	71	5	.	20	.	30	21	30	David Thompson
2	124	5	.	20	.	29	35	96	Thomas Roberson
3	53	5	.	20	.	21	10	60	Saml. Leatherwood
4	50	5	.	20	.	20	10	00	Thomas Roberson
5	56	5	.	20	.	20	11	20	Wm. H. Thomas
6	134	5	.	20	1	80	241	20	Fran. McGee
7	267	4	.	50	7	00	1869	00	Eli Ledford
8	78	5	.	20	.	25	19	50	Ezekiel Dowdle
9	143	5	.	20	3	00	429	00	Berry Howke
10	128	4	.	50	7	02	898	56	do. do.
11	157	5	.	20	1	00	157	00	David Copenning
12	365	2	2	00	15	42	5628	30	do do
13	86	5	.	20	2	05	176	30	John Saunders
14	82	5	.	20	.	70	57	40	Joseph Kilpatrick
15	222	5	.	20	.	20	44	40	John W. Davis
16	155	3	1	00	10	95	1697	25	Saml. Jarvis
17	122	5	.	20	.	85	103	70	Saml. Jarvis
18	212	5	.	20	.	58	122	96	Wm. M. Davis
19	112	5	.	20	.	20	22	40	Wm. H. Thomas
20	130	2	2	00	9	56	1242	80	Joseph Cockrum
21	180	5	.	20	.	82	147	60	do do
22	94	5	.	20	.	20	18	80	Wm. H. Thomas
23	71	5	.	20	.	82	58	22	Douglas Davis
24	245	5	.	20	.	20	49	00	do do
25	50	5	.	20	.				
26	174	5	.	20	1	00	174	00	Wm. M. Davis
27	143	2	2	00	10	06	1438	58	John Moore
28	68	5	.	20	2	01	136	68	Wm. M. Davis
29	90	3	1	00	7	00	630	00	Richard Edminston

Sales summary of 1838 Cherokee lands surveyed by Robert Henry, Folder 1, Volume 1, Scan 8, in the Cherokee Lands Sales books, #1966-z. *Southern Historical Collection, Wilson Library, University of North Carolina at Chapel Hill.*

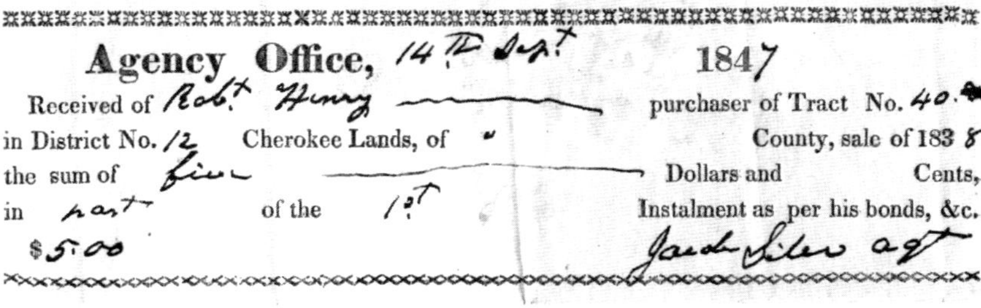

Agency Office, 14th Sept 1847
Received of Robt Henry purchaser of Tract No. 40.
in District No. 12 Cherokee Lands, of " County, sale of 1838
the sum of five Dollars and Cents,
in part of the 1st Instalment as per his bonds, &c.
$5.00 Jacob Siler agt

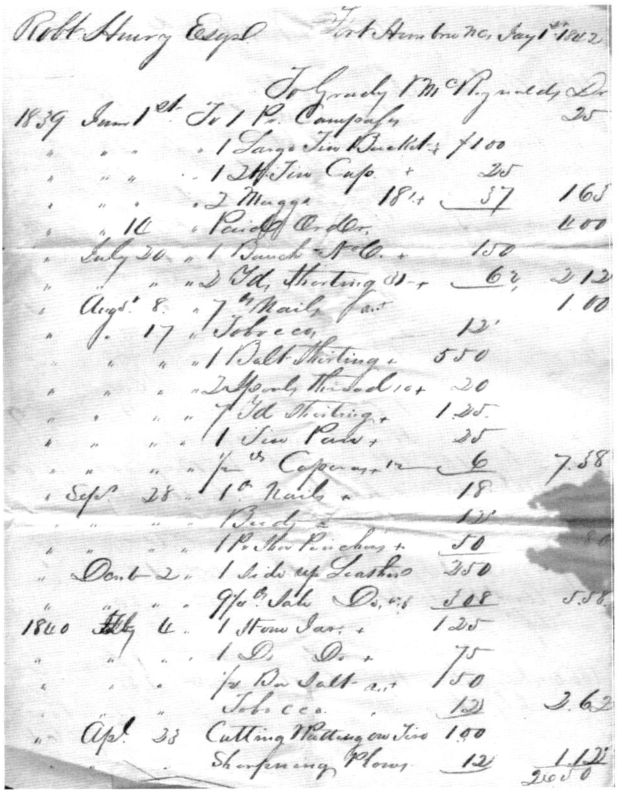

Robt Henry Esqr Fort Hembree NC, Jany 1st 1842
To Grady & McReynolds Dr
1839 Jan 1st To 1 Pr. Campasses 25
1 Large Tin Bucket 1.00
1 Tin Cup 25
2 Muggs 18 37 1.63
10 Paid Order 4.00
July 20 1 Bunch ... 1.50
2 Yd Shirting 31 62 2.12
Augt 8 7 lb Nails 1.00
17 Tobacco 12
1 Bolt Shirting 5.50
2 Spools Thread 10 20
1 Yd Shirting 1.25
1 Tin Pan 25
... 6 7.58
Sept 28 1 lb Nails 18
... 12
1 Pr Shoe Pinchers 50
Oct 2 1 Side up Leather 2.50
... Salt 3.08 5.58
1840 Feby 6 1 Stone Jar 1.25
1 Do Do 75
Bu Salt 1.50
Tobacco 12 3.62
Apl 23 Cutting ... 1.00
Sharpening Plows 12 1.12
20.50

Above: Robert purchased some of the same land he had surveyed before the removal of the Cherokees. *Henry Archive (private collection).*

Right: Robert Henry's itemized debits and credits for goods and services purchased from Grady and McReynolds, dated January 1, 1842. *Henry Archive (private collection).*

months and was then employed in the area until the land sales. North Carolina and Tennessee troops moved approximately one thousand Cherokee into Fort Hembree.[155] One wonders if Robert Henry witnessed the long columns of distraught Cherokee neighbors who had been forced from their nearby homes.

By the end of June, the Cherokee had been removed, and the fort was empty. Having served its purpose, it was abandoned, and its buildings were eventually converted and purposed for other uses. A store and post office operated on the premises until the founding of Hayesville in 1861.

Robert continued his farming and added a mill. He was joined by one of Reuben's longtime hired hands, Abraham Fullbright. Fullbright, accompanied by a family slave named George, assisted Henry with his first crop. Fullbright also brought with him fifty dollars for Henry's use that had been allocated from Henry and Deaver's Sulphur Spring account.

Cherokee lands were first offered for sale in September 1838.[156] Henry, already familiar with the prime tracts, quickly entered claims for hundreds of acres, including several tracts on the banks of Tusquittee and Compass Creeks.

Returning to Buncombe County for a short while, he filed claims for more land along the French Broad River. While in Buncombe, he spent his time at the Sulphur Springs Hotel, along with his servants, sons, unmarried daughter and William G. Tidwell and Eliza Henry Tidwell. He may have also brought his slave "Old Julia" and her grandchildren, Ham, Sarah and John, with him.[157]

Reuben Deaver was also back in Buncombe County, managing the Sulphur Springs and serving as postmaster. He completed several Buncombe County surveys in November and December 1840 as well.[158]

By the time of the June 1, 1840 federal census, Robert had returned to and settled in his new home near Compass Creek, now in the newly formed county of Cherokee. Robert periodically received homespun clothes from his daughter, Polly Deaver. Polly was a champion spinner, and when nine years old, on a spinning wheel on Grassy Creek in Buncombe County, had spun more thread than did the daughter of local Judge Burton.[159]

Chapter 11

Trouble in Paradise

[Tidwell] *was a drunkard, a gambler...and was suspected to have occasioned the death of his first wife.*

The spring of 1844 was a trying time for Robert Henry. He appeared a successful man, accomplished in all his undertakings over many decades. He was a wealthy man, a seasoned and brilliant attorney, a renowned surveyor and an owner of thousands of acres of prime real estate. He had supervised and financed a prosperous business venture and was living his later years in a beautiful area of western North Carolina. It should have been a time of rest, reflection and tranquility.

But the reality was much different. His family was being torn apart, his business alliance with Reuben Deaver was crumbling and prolonged legal battles loomed on the horizon. His marriage to Dorcas, from whom he had been separated for many years, would come to an end. In addition, his favorite daughter, Polly Deaver, died in April of that year.

Robert's longstanding drinking habit had become progressively worse, affecting both his business and personal life. While gentle and kind when sober, he could be cruel and verbally abusive in his inebriated state. In 1836, in the midst of one of his drunken tirades, he had commanded his wife to leave his house, an order with which she complied. In 1842, Dorcas Bell petitioned for divorce in the Haywood County Superior Court of Law, and in the spring of 1844, the jury found in her favor on all counts. The defendant, Robert Henry, had "maliciously turned plaintiff out of doors" and made her "condition burdensome and life intolerable." Dorcas asked no alimony, only that she may be divorced *a mensa et thoro* (from bed and board), giving her property and contract rights. Robert was ordered to pay full court costs.[160]

A bitter feud between Robert Henry and Reuben Deaver had been brewing for years. The once-enthusiastic partners could not resolve their differences on a number of financial and personal matters. Reuben was uneasy with their arrangement and had been in want of a new settlement since 1835. He later stated he feared he would receive "no justice until deceased," and indeed, it would take many years for any resolution of his concerns.[161]

One solution to their grievances would be to sell the Sulphur Springs. In fact, Reuben had already tried. In a *Charleston Courier* advertisement on July 11, 1839, he stated, "P.S. For private reasons (not for the want of custom), the proprietor expects during this season to offer the above property for sale, either in part or in the whole." Later, traveling to Robert's home in Cherokee County in October 1844, Deaver secured a power of attorney allowing him to sell the springs for no less than $15,000. Sometime after 1844, Deaver again went to Cherokee. This time, the sale price would not be less than $33,000, with one third each for Robert Henry, his children and Deaver.

Their plans to sell either failed or were dropped, so Henry and Deaver agreed to resolve their differences using a panel of arbitrators. On November 2, 1847, Joshua Roberts, Nimion Edmunston, Charles Moore and Joseph Keener met at the Sulphur Springs Hotel to begin the arduous task of sifting through stacks of documents to find an equitable solution.[162] For the next three weeks, the men examined account ledgers and business receipts, estimated property values and improvement costs and determined the value of family slaves.

On November 25, the initial decision was made and then amended slightly due to exceptions by Deaver and Henry in April 1848. The Sulphur Springs plantation (except for improvements made by Reuben), mills and slaves reverted to Robert Henry, as per their 1833 agreement. After a thorough review and comparison of Deaver and Henry's books, the arbitrators concluded that Reuben owed Robert over $4,400. This he would have to pay by November 1849.

However, Reuben's improvements were valued at over $11,000 and belonged to him. His award included land adjacent to and encompassing the area of the hotel buildings and the springs, which were ruled as necessary for the enjoyment and occupancy of his improvements. Henry had a choice: pay the money owed Deaver within two years, or surrender the improvements and associated property to him. If Robert chose the latter option, Reuben could not prevent the use of the Sulphur Springs and its water by Henry.

It is not surprising that neither party was satisfied with the arbitrators' awards. The 1848 amendments were not satisfactory to Reuben, who believed they favored Henry. He felt a failed partnership with Robert's son, Robert M. Henry, had not been taken into consideration. He charged that certain relevant receipts had been burned by Dorcas Bell Henry and that there was more unfinished business that was damaging to him.

However, Henry believed that the arbitrators' awards favored his son-in-law. He claimed Deaver kept his books with the design to defraud him from the very beginning, that the entry book given to the arbitrators was different than the one Robert had originally seen in 1833 and that it had several pages missing from the front. He knew of no partnership with Robert M. Henry nor of any burning of receipts by his wife, a charge that she denied. He stated that because Dorcas could not read, Deaver may somehow have deceived her into burning them without her knowledge.

Reuben called for another meeting of the arbitrators. In a letter to Robert dated June 1, 1848, Deaver said he had heard from respectable sources that Henry had told arbitrator Edmunston not to attend a June 3 meeting. He suggested that Henry might agree to replace Edmunston with another person.

The information Deaver had obtained was a falsehood, Henry replied, stating that he had twice tried to get Edmunston to attend. He would not agree to replace an arbitrator with one who had no knowledge of the facts, but offered, "If you will agree to dismiss the whole of the arbitrators and choose others who are all equally ignorant of the past transactions, I will agree to that." On June 3, when Edmunston did not appear for the meeting, as Deaver had suspected, he dismissed the arbitrators and decided to take Henry up on his offer. The documents of the initial arbitration process were left for safekeeping in the care of neighbor Charles Moore, one of the first arbitrators.

Two years later, no resolution was in sight. Robert now lived in Cherokee County with his daughter Eliza Tidwell Moore; her husband, Narboone W. Moore; and Eliza's children from her marriage to William G. Tidwell. Robert's ex-wife, Dorcas Bell, was living with their son William L. Henry on the Sulphur Springs plantation near the mills. Robert had taken possession of the farmland and mills via William, excepting some houses and about five acres but including the yard, garden and a grove Deaver had procured from Charles Moore.

However, Reuben had not surrendered the Sulphur Springs complex. In 1850, he was still living at the hotel with Mary Torian, his new wife of three years; daughters Eugenia and Louisa from his first marriage; children Rebecca and Nat from his second marriage; and William Deaver, age eighty-seven.[163]

Unknown to Reuben, Henry had collected the unfinished arbitrators' papers, left two years previous with Charles Moore, and taken them to the Cherokee County Superior Court of Law. In an effort to force Deaver to pay the $4,400 due him, he claimed the award was final and conclusive. It appeared to Reuben there was only one option left for him, so he filed a legal complaint of his own. On March 18, 1851, Robert Henry received a summons requiring him to appear before the Buncombe County Court of Equity. He and Dorcas Bell Henry were being sued by Reuben Deaver.

At the 1851 spring term, the first (but not the last) court battle for control of Sulphur Springs began. All of Henry and Deaver's business dealings and relationships came into dispute. Testimony was received from friends, relatives, neighbors and business associates. Accusations, mistruths, exaggerations, misunderstandings and fabrications swirled like fall leaves in the wind.

First, the manner in which the two had initially contemplated their joint business and came to sign the 1833 articles of agreement was in dispute. Deaver testified that he had traveled to Tennessee in 1830 or 1831, after his marriage to Polly Henry, under the assumption that he and Polly were going to receive land from Robert Love. But in 1831, when preparing to move to the Western Country, Robert Henry offered him part of his Sulphur Springs land. Samuel Fitzgerald, a witness for Deaver, substantiated the claim, and Joseph Deaver, Reuben's brother, testified that upon their return from Tennessee, Henry had indeed discovered the springs and made Reuben and Polly the offer.

Robert Henry labeled this claim a "foul fabrication," and Dorcas Bell also denied its occurrence. He and Deaver had instead gone together to Tennessee to view five hundred acres that would be a gift to him and Dorcas, not Deaver, if they were to remove west. The land would come from a partial division of lands held by Robert Love in partnership with his son, Thomas Love. It was when the land did not suit Henry that they returned to Carolina, had discussions and decided to live together with their families and take in boarders. Robert said that at the time, Deaver had only two or three horses and a pair of oxen and was indebted in Charleston for $2,000, so he furnished him with funds to discharge the debt and begin a store.

Yes, there had been a joint trip to Tennessee, Deaver countered, but not as described by Henry. They went to Tennessee in order to collect several thousand dollars owed to Henry, and when collected, it would be appropriated to the buildings and improvements at the Sulphur Springs.

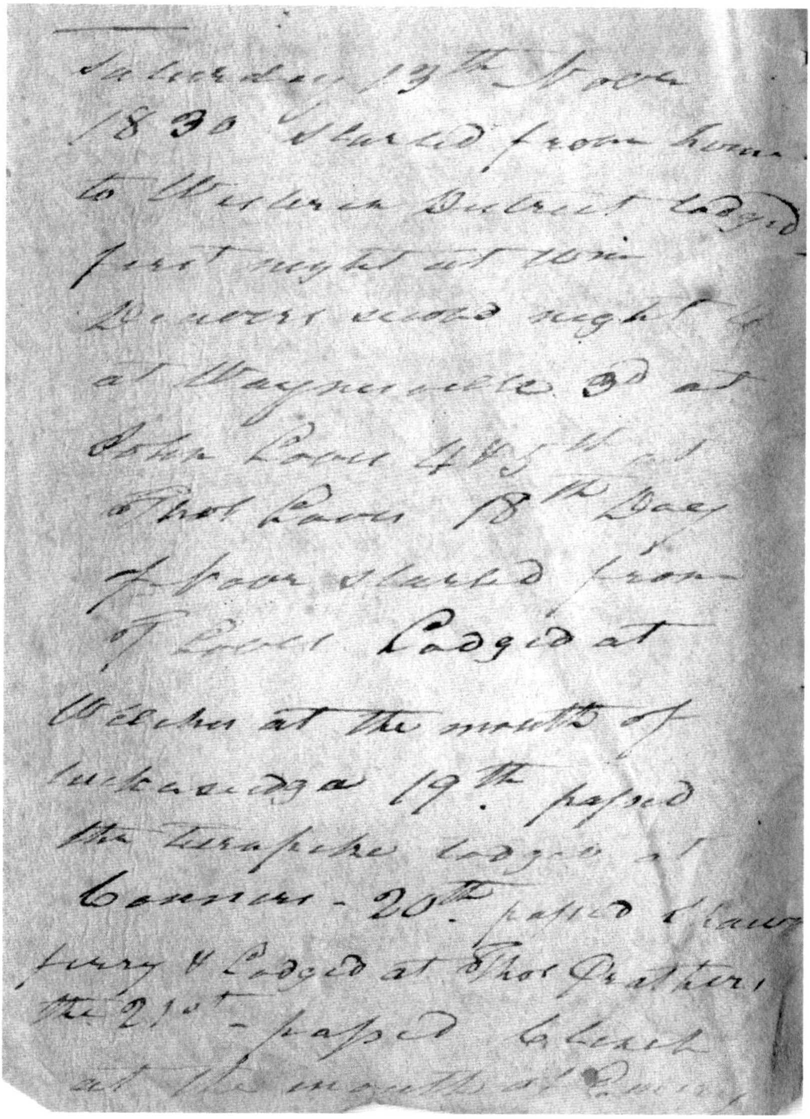
Saturday 13th Nove
1830 Started from home
to Western District Lodged
first night at Wm
Deavers second night
at Waynesville 3d at
John Loves 4th & 5th at
Thos Loves 18th Day
of Nove started from
T Loves Lodged at
Webbers at the mouth of
Tuckasedga 19th passed
the Turnpike Lodged at
Conners - 20th passed Clay
ferry & Lodged at Thos Prathers
the 21st - passed Creek
at the mouth of

Robert documented his 1830 Tennessee trip to the Western Country. *Henry Archive (private collection).*

Witness Fitzgerald stated that Reuben's first trip to Tennessee was with Colonel Love and occurred in 1830. However, entries in a Robert Henry notebook detail a November and December 1830 journey to the Western District with Deaver, staying at Thomas Love's for the fourth and fifth days. Robert's horse "took the thumps and lock jaw," so on December 2, he "sent back to James Love's, who lived 16 miles from Columbia, for a horse, and Reuben went to N. Deaver's." The notebook did not indicate whether any money had been collected.

Reuben said he had not been satisfied with the 1833 arrangement as early as 1835. A new agreement and will were drawn up by Henry, but the papers were taken from him in 1837 when Henry went to Cherokee. Henry said he was the one who wanted a settlement with his partner and not a new contract because he was "tired of him" and that Deaver had put it off for a year.

Reuben expected and believed that he was promised reimbursement for his expenses. He spent a considerable amount of his own money and entered into business contracts even before the formal agreement. Henry's family constantly took goods from the store, he charged, for which he did not receive sufficient reimbursement.

In another area of contention, Reuben complained that Henry's offer had included giving him the farm and any improvements he made as an advancement to Polly upon their marriage and also that he had promised part of the springs property to his other daughter Eliza and her husband, William G. Tidwell. Robert had described how he wanted to divide the springs property between Deaver and Tidwell, his sons-in-law. Deaver was to receive the improvements and Tidwell the remainder, including the principal farm and mills. It was in anticipation of these terms that Henry drew up the 1833 articles of agreement, Reuben said, and he believed this arrangement was designed to induce Tidwell into a business partnership.

Robert left deeds, receipts and a will with Reuben describing this division of land and then later, Deaver claimed, took possession of the papers under the "pretense" of making new deeds and did not return them.

He did not make a will, Robert said, except for one time when he was having trouble with a man that may have terminated seriously. That will was destroyed on resolution of the problem. As to deeds and receipts, Robert denied giving them to Deaver, saying that Deaver himself had taken them from his unlocked chest when he removed to Cherokee.

J.R. Love, a witness for Deaver, stated that it was true that Henry had intended the springs for Deaver's and Tidwell's wives, but only until Polly Deaver died in 1844. Other witnesses had participated in or overheard conversations in which Robert talked many times of his intention to his convey property to Polly in his will, and that any transfer would not occur while he was living.

Deaver said that Henry did not pretend existence of their contract until after the death of Polly in 1844, but Henry vowed he had always thought their agreement was in force. He said he never promised Deaver the plantation and that it was not in the agreement. Deaver was to have any houses or houses built, or their value, but not any property, and any sums he gave to him were loans. Any sharing of the buildings and profits before the agreement were only "experiments," and not in writing. Therefore, certain sums of money and expenses Deaver thought were his were not included.

Robert had no recollection of plans to divide any lands between his sons-in-law and believed Deaver's claim of a Tidwell partnership was false because he (Robert) did not care for the character of Tidwell. He testified that Reuben once returned from a trip to South Carolina during which he had a chance to inquire of Tidwell's character. Deaver told him it was "first rate," so the marriage of Eliza Henry and Tidwell took place. The true character though, according to Henry, was that Tidwell was "a drunkard, a gambler, and extremely cruel and was suspected to have occasioned the death of his first wife." He fervently believed Eliza's husbands were "spendthrifts being part of their faults," so much so that he later included the charge in his will. Also, Robert stated, the agreement in question was dated 1833, and the marriage of his daughter to Tidwell did not occur until the May 14, 1835. Dorcas Bell Henry added that Eliza and Tidwell had not even met by the time of the agreement. Robert said that his only proposal to Tidwell was that he may live in the house and work the plantation and mill.

Although Henry denied suggesting the partnership in the first place, as Deaver charged, he did have an opinion on its dissolution. Tidwell had confided in Henry that he thought Deaver would cheat him (Tidwell) out of all he owned and that he would "not leave worth a dressed buckskin," and for that reason, Tidwell ended his partnership. Deaver said the partnership lasted until Tidwell had a disagreement with Polly Henry's family, and that was the real reason Tidwell was prompted to leave.

A third area of dispute was the monetary value of the Henry and Love family slaves placed under the control of Deaver. Many were sold or taken back by Robert or his wife, and those who remained were an expense to him, Deaver said. In 1836, Reuben considered their contract abandoned when he lost the services of several slaves, notifying Robert that it was time for a settlement. Henry said Dorcas did not take slaves with her that year and that there remained Harriet, Dublin and Andy, as well as his "old stock" of Julia, Sam, Jack and John. He stated that none were taken until after the arbitrators' award.

Julia was an "aged woman who worked for herself" but was fed and clothed by him, Deaver stated. While described as an "old woman of little value" by

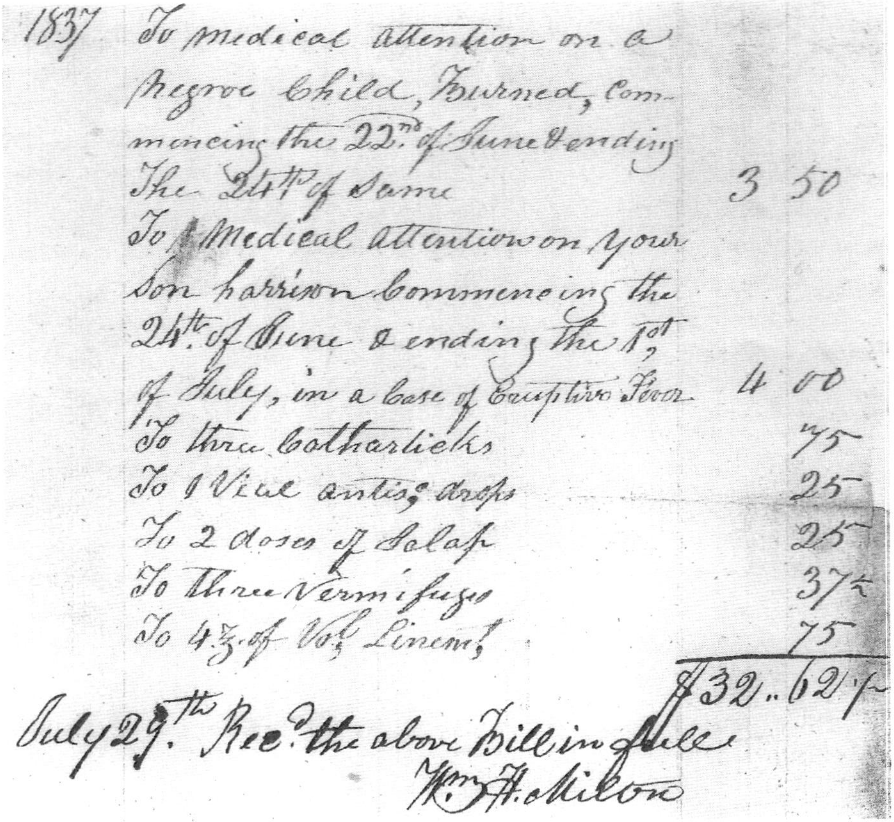

1837 To medical attention on a Negroe Child, Burned, Commencing the 22nd of June & ending The 24th of same — 3 50
To Medical attention on your Son harrison Commencing the 24th. of June & ending the 1st, of July, in a case of Eruptive Fever — 4 00
To three Cathartics — 75
To 1 Vial antis. drops — 25
To 2 doses of Jalap — 25
To three Vermifuges — 37½
To 4 ʒ of Vol. Linem. — 75
$32..62½
July 29th. Recd. the above Bill in full
Wm. H. Milton

Receipt for medical attention for a burned slave and the illness of Harrison Deaver, son of Reuben. *North Carolina Department of Archives and History.*

Deaver, defendant Henry felt there were "few black women better in the field or at home." Julia's daughter Malinda (Lynn) had two children who were twins. One died of burns, while the other, named Catherine, was a young girl of seventeen, "and small at that." According to Deaver, "The girl Lynn was given to my wife verbally, but after having three more children, Mr. Henry sent her to Tidwell in South Carolina in 1836, leaving me to raise the children without the mother until they were just large enough to begin to do something, when they were taken with Old Julia by Mr. Henry to Cherokee in 1837."

John, who was aged five or six in 1831, was taken to Cherokee in 1837. John was a valuable man. Robert Henry commented that John could throw a shovelful of clay eighteen feet out of the race channel when it was being dug. But Deaver complained he had "learnt him to be a meat cook" and then had to pay "hire for him at common price."

Sam the ostler, or stableman, was a young known as a good hand. Jack, a "yellow boy," whom Reuben had instructed in carpentry, was taken to Cherokee in 1841 by Henry, and when he left, he carried with him "a good site of tools." Jack was sold in 1843. Ben was a "simple boy" who was raised and fed for several years before being sold.

Old Man Dublin (Dub) was with Deaver until 1846, except for about a year and a half around 1836, when he was taken by Mrs. Henry, after which time he found his way back to Deaver's. Deaver claimed he was lame. Henry agreed but stated that he was still an asset because he was "in the prime of life."

Dorcas Henry owned three "young and raw half hands" named Jim, Hannah and Andrew. Andrew was noted as even stouter than John by Robert Henry. He and Hannah, always known as Mrs. Henry's waiting girl, were removed to Haywood County in 1836 with Mrs. Henry.

When slave Jim killed a horse, Mr. Henry and all the rest of the hands said he must be sold. In 1835, Deaver recalled, Dorcas Henry consented to sell two slaves, Jim and Harriet, to a trader for $1,100 via James R. Love, general agent for her father. The proceeds were to be given to Deaver in lieu of the slaves, but Dorcas kept the money and in 1837 instructed Deaver to purchase a "negroe" for his wife. Deaver thought he was still owed $640 for his purchase, but it was not awarded by the arbitrators.

Robert stated that since Dorcas, a "femme covert," was separated from him at the time, she had no legal authority to sell the slaves without his consent. He had nothing to do with the sale, as the slaves had come by the hand of his wife, and therefore the transaction itself was void. Robert Love had advanced him and Dorcas a slave named Sal upon their marriage in 1814 who became the mother of Jim, Andy and Harriet, a mulatto. In 1820, with the advice and consent of Robert Love, Robert sold Sal and her children to Dillard Love. Dillard did not pay, so in 1827, Robert received Jim, Andy and their sister Hannah. Then, in 1832, Harriet was returned. Deaver complained that after Lynn and Hannah were taken, he had no servants to cook or wash, yet the sons still remained there.

The sale was detailed in the later court testimony of James R. Love, Dorcas's brother. James had partnered with his sister and sold Jim and Harriet for $1,100. James did not know if Mr. Henry agreed to the sale or was present for it, as Henry was always "moping about." Dorcas received the money, but all parties agreed it should go to Deaver. When the money was received, Deaver was to use it to purchase a slave for his wife and one for Tidwell's wife, Eliza. Love thought Dorcas had allowed Deaver to pay too much for his wife's slave, but Dorcas said that it was her money and she

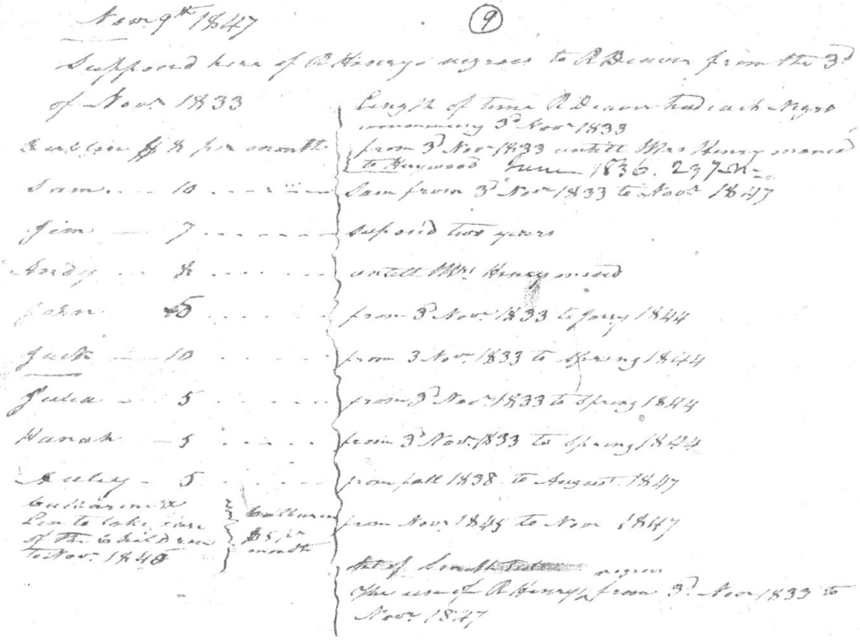

The Henry family slaves were rented to Reuben Deaver and considered a cost of business. *North Carolina Department of Archives and History.*

could do with it as she pleased. However, Deaver said that when the Deaver-Tidwell partnership went sour, Dorcas directed him to take the money and use it to pay off Tidwell for goods he had purchased in Charleston.

Henry and Deaver battled over every detail of their partnership. Originally, Reuben was obligated to supply Robert Henry's family in "victuals" and clothing, except for Robert Henry's two sons. But, Reuben said, Robert was there much of the time in 1840 with his horses and servants, as well as William Tidwell and Eliza Henry Tidwell, all living at the house. The drinking board was kept full, and Robert would entertain his friends for a week at a time with no charge. Although separated from Robert, Dorcas was there often with her servants and son Robert M. Henry. All were an expense to him, Deaver claimed.

The Henry family contributed much to the venture, according to Robert. Recalling Deaver's use of his family's services, he said Reuben "may have just as well stated he had use of the family as slaves, the only distinction being that of color."

Another partnership, this one with Robert M. Henry, had not been considered by the arbitrators, Reuben complained. In 1841, Robert had proposed Reuben reengage in selling retail goods and that if he would take in his son as a partner, he would contribute $2,000. Reuben agreed and borrowed $2,500 from a Georgia man, hoping for the best. A large stock of goods was purchased in the name of Henry and Deaver with the money, but when the loan came due, the elder Robert failed to pay. He instead said he had sold a tract of land and had other notes that were to be collected and could be used to effect payment. The notes were placed in the hands of his son Robert M. Henry for collection.

According to Reuben, whenever notes were given to R.M. Henry, he returned either with less than expected or with an excuse that the party was "insolvent." It wasn't long before Robert M. withdrew from the partnership, leaving Deaver with all the debts. The elder Henry replied that he was unaware of the partnership, of which he was displeased, until long after it had begun. His son had requested a loan of $2,000, but he refused to loan him the money. He had a note of $1,000 he could have if it was collected, but it had never been recovered. Furthermore, Henry said, he was informed the partnership had made money but that none was ever given to his son, who then decided to read law in Waynesville.

Perhaps most important in the deliberations had been placing an estimated value on the hotel, buildings and other improvements. The less the improvements were worth, the less Deaver would potentially be owed by Henry. Several witnesses testified that the hotel, plantation and springs were in a general state of disrepair at the time Deaver took control and that he had made vast changes and improvements. Although construction had begun before Deaver first arrived, Henry claimed the dam was built in the wrong location and prone to repairs. He also believed the hotel was now so run down that the improvements were not worth as much as Deaver stated. His witnesses testified to finding rotting wood, chimneys separating from the building and doors that would not close. In addition, the meadow was overgrown.

Approximations of the hotel's value varied widely, depending with whom the evaluator's loyalty was placed and his level of qualification. On November 24, 1847, William Francis completed a very detailed estimate of building materials and cost of labor, determining a value between $11,000 and $12,000.

A number of expenses in Henry and Deaver's entry books, some bordering on trivial, were also argued. Henry stated that Deaver charged him two dollars for a handsaw he had actually purchased before the agreement and that he claimed one dollar for a razor requested by slave Jack to shave boarders, which had been Henry's. When Deaver purchased two looking glasses for the hotel sitting room, Dorcas wanted two of her own.

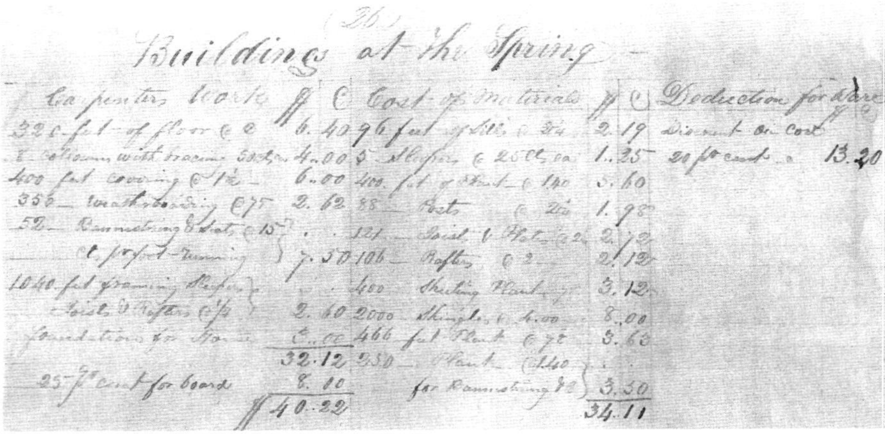

Estimate of the replacement value of the buildings at the springs. *North Carolina Department of Archives and History.*

Deaver complied with her request and made the purchase. One looking glass was either broken by Deaver or was broken in some other way before it was received by Dorcas, but a charge of fourteen dollars appeared for it in Deaver's entry book. Robert stated that Deaver charged him for furniture taken from the store by Henry's daughters on their marriage but that the furniture was from his personal residence and had been made by his nieces to pay for their board. Deaver charged him for fifty head of hogs, most of which had belonged to Henry's stock. Many had died on a drive from a discontinued stillhouse business near the Pigeon River to Cherokee County, but the charge was still for the entire fifty head.

Deaver said he did not get a sum of money due from William D. Smith, even though it was recorded that he had. In 1839 or 1840, John B. Love testified that he paid Robert Henry $223 received from Peyton Wells but that Henry had tried to get him to say he had paid it to Deaver. In court, Henry questioned if Love had not, in fact, destroyed the receipt to prevent its introduction as evidence to the arbitrators, a charge that Love denied.

In December 1841, because "difficulties arose," Reuben entered for a state grant of thirty-six acres that would run diagonally through the Sulphur Springs plantation and include two-thirds of the house and improvements.[164] This he did, saying later that it was only to "secure his interests" and that when he offered the grant to Henry, he would not take the deed.

Polly L. Deaver, wife of R. Deaver & daughter of R. & D. Henry, died on Saturday about 9 o'clock p.m. on the 6th of April 1844.

It wasn't long after Polly's death in 1844 that Reuben tried once more to exit the agreement. He again attempted to sell the springs and eight hundred acres, placing an advertisement in the *Charleston Courier* in October 1844, the sale "not caused by any discouragement, but owing to a providential loss" in his family. He would take private bids until the next November, when the legislature met in Charleston, at which point he would meet with prospective purchasers. He was willing to take one-fourth of the purchase price within six months and allow one, two and three years or longer for the balance, "and a part would be taken in negro property if desired." As a service to the buyer, he would stay on for another season to help. He did make it clear, however, that if he did not sell, he would be back next year to carry on business as usual, with more improvements. He was not successful in this effort.

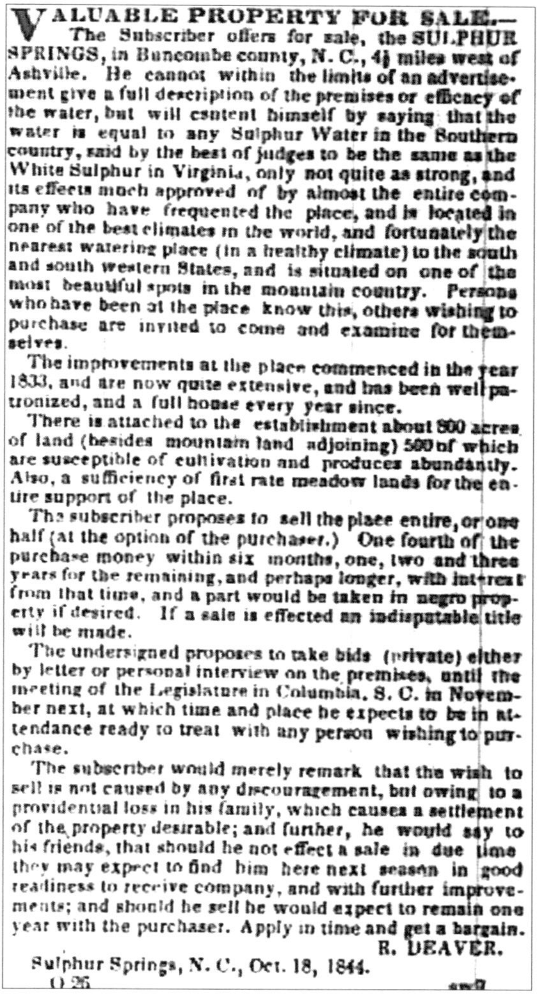

VALUABLE PROPERTY FOR SALE.—The Subscriber offers for sale, the SULPHUR SPRINGS, in Buncombe county, N. C., 4½ miles west of Ashville. He cannot within the limits of an advertisement give a full description of the premises or efficacy of the water, but will content himself by saying that the water is equal to any Sulphur Water in the Southern country, said by the best of judges to be the same as the White Sulphur in Virginia, only not quite as strong, and its effects much approved of by almost the entire company who have frequented the place, and is located in one of the best climates in the world, and fortunately the nearest watering place (in a healthy climate) to the south and south western States, and is situated on one of the most beautiful spots in the mountain country. Persons who have been at the place know this, others wishing to purchase are invited to come and examine for themselves.

The improvements at the place commenced in the year 1833, and are now quite extensive, and has been well patronized, and a full house every year since.

There is attached to the establishment about 800 acres of land (besides mountain land adjoining) 500 of which are susceptible of cultivation and produces abundantly. Also, a sufficiency of first rate meadow lands for the entire support of the place.

The subscriber proposes to sell the place entire, or one half (at the option of the purchaser.) One fourth of the purchase money within six months, one, two and three years for the remaining, and perhaps longer, with interest from that time, and a part would be taken in negro property if desired. If a sale is effected an indisputable title will be made.

The undersigned proposes to take bids (private) either by letter or personal interview on the premises, until the meeting of the Legislature in Columbia, S. C. in November next, at which time and place he expects to be in attendance ready to treat with any person wishing to purchase.

The subscriber would merely remark that the wish to sell is not caused by any discouragement, but owing to a providential loss in his family, which causes a settlement of the property desirable; and further, he would say to his friends, that should he not effect a sale in due time they may expect to find him here next season in good readiness to receive company, and with further improvements; and should he sell he would expect to remain one year with the purchaser. Apply in time and get a bargain.

R. DEAVER.

Sulphur Springs, N. C., Oct. 18, 1844.

O 26 swf

The effort to sell Sulphur Springs ended in failure. *Charleston Courier*, October 26, 1844. *South Caroliniana Library.*

Polly's death was a turning point for Robert Henry. He no longer spoke of giving land or improvements to his son-in-law.[165] His daughter was gone, and he was no longer fond of Deaver. But Reuben had the force of a legal document, stating, "I have been much damaged and outrageously treated, something like a perfect tool for others." Sooner or later, he intended to receive justice.

According the first arbitrators' ruling, Henry could elect to pay Reuben over $11,000 for the improvements within two years, or surrender them. Robert believed that he was not required to lay off the springs lands to Deaver until Deaver paid him the $4,400 awarded him, and that had not been done. Reuben had surrendered the plantation, mills and slaves to Robert's son William L. Henry, who lived on the land near the mills, but had retained the springs and other improvements and continued living at the hotel. He had even leased another portion of the plantation from William L. Henry and hired some of the Henry family slaves.

In February 1852, Reuben was still living at the springs. He had been there since the arbitration decision in November 1847 and, in fact, had been there since the building of the hotel twenty years previous. His son was born in the original boarding "corner house," and his first wife died there. His father, brother and second wife, Mary Torian, also made the hotel their home.

In a tragic turn of events, on May 23, 1852, Reuben Deaver died, not quite forty-five years of age, leaving no will. He was buried at the Sulphur Springs Cemetery. Reuben was dead, but the case of *Deaver v. Henry* was very much alive. Joshua Roberts, one of the arbitrators, became the administrator of Reuben's estate and continued the lawsuit.

> *Reuben Deaver died at the Sulphur Springs on the 23rd of May 1852 at 7 a.m. on Sunday.*
>
> *Widow Polly Deaver* [Mary Torian] *started from the Sulphur Springs to her father's with her family & a wagon well loaded on the 15th* [of September] *1852.*

The case was continued in the court several times, with a final stop at the North Carolina Supreme Court in 1853. The court commented that both parties kept their books in a disorganized manner, but it used most of the calculations made by the first arbitrators. The court ruled in favor of Deaver. Henry took possession of Deaver's improvements in April, for which he would have to pay $4,707.69. He was ordered to pay all Supreme Court costs, one half of attorney fees ($200.00) and all Buncombe County court costs. After exceptions and more depositions, the award was decreased to $4,387.21. The case had finally been resolved, but Reuben had not lived to see the conclusion.

Operation of the hotel and springs was back in the Henry family. The name Deaver's Sulphur Springs was retained for a time before being changed

SULPHUR SPRINGS, N. C.—The undersigned respectfully inform the travelling public, in search of health or pleasure, that they have taken charge of the Hotel at SULPHUR SPRINGS, near Asheville, N. C., and are having it fitted up with entire NEW FURNITURE, and will open it on the 1st day of July for the entertainment of visitors.

There is attached to the Hotel a large dancing Saloon, which will be furnished with a splendid Band of Music.

Their charges will be reasonable. They hope by diligence, and their exertions to please, to be able to furnish as good, if not better, accommodations than have ever been found in the above establishment heretofore.

R. HENRY & SONS.

Sulphur Springs, N. C., June 2, 1853.

Ju 7 tu4

Above: The Henry family regained control of the Sulphur Springs. *Charleston Courier*, June 14, 1853. *South Caroliniana Library.*

Right: *Asheville News*, July 6, 1854. *North Carolina Collection, Pack Memorial Public Library, Asheville, NC.*

SULPHUR SPRINGS,
BUNCOMBE COUNTY, N. C.

William L. Henry having become sole proprietor of this well known watering place, takes this method of announcing to the public, that the House will be open for the reception of visitors the 1st day of June next. Having fitted up the house and furnished with new and elegant furniture, and having provided himself with polite and accommodating servants, he hopes by strict attention to the wants and wishes of his guests to give general satisfaction His table shall be furnished with the very best the country affords.—While his stables are large and commodious, will be supplied with grain and provender and attended by faithful and attentive Ostlers. A first rate band of music will be in attendance all the time. In short no pains or expense will be spared to render a sojourn at the springs pleasant and agreeable, and the proprietor hopes by unremitting attention to the comfort of his guests to secure a continuation of the patronage heretofore so liberally bestowed on the springs; assuring all who may visit the Springs for health or pleasure that they will find the accommodations at least equal to what it has heretofore been.

He deems it unnecessary to say anything in regard to the Medicinal qualities of the Sulphur Springs, as they have been so long and so favorably known, and their healing virtues tested by hundreds and thousands who have visited them in years past.

A comfortable hack with safe horses and an experienced driver, will run daily between the Springs and Asheville, affording those who may arrive at Asheville by stage a certain means of going and returning from the Spring at pleasure.

WILLIAM L. HENRY.

June 1, 1854. 1m.

to Sulphur Springs. William L. Henry took over management duties, which were later hired out to third parties. An August 14, 1858 advertisement in the *Asheville Spectator* announced that Thomas Goodlake had "taken charge of this celebrated watering place." Goodlake also kept up his own stables, carriage shop and blacksmith shop in Asheville where, he said, "horses, hacks and buggies can be had at any hour."

Chapter 12

The Twilight Years

Undoubtedly the last of the heroes of Kings Mountain.[166]

In 1837, Robert Henry was living and farming near Tusquittee Creek in western North Carolina. It seems he was always comfortable with life in a new frontier. He had done it before, and this would be another new start. He could tend to his farm, build a mill, do a little surveying and continue a leisurely life of reading, traveling and enjoying his new surroundings. The Sulphur Springs Hotel and plantation were in the hands of Reuben Deaver at the time, so he assumed he need not worry about that. Occasionally, he would go back to the springs, staying at the hotel, accompanied by an entourage of friends, family and slaves.

Robert was now seventy years old and was becoming one of the last of his generation. Revolutionary War veterans and boundary-line runners David Vance and William McDowell, traveling companion William MacLean and friend Israel Pickens had all passed away. By 1845, Robert's sisters Margaret, Jane and Rachel; brothers John and Joseph; daughter Polly Deaver; and father-in-law, Robert Love, had all died.

Always the speculator, Robert entered claims for land, obtained additional grants and sold bits and pieces of his North Carolina holdings in Cherokee, Macon, Henderson and Buncombe Counties. He purchased two parcels of land totaling 276 acres from Benjamin S. Matlock in Cherokee County in 1840.[167] In 1846, probably not able to make the journey himself any longer, he sent son William to sell 360 acres on the Forked Deer River in Madison County, Tennessee.

When Robert first went to his Cherokee land in 1837, his slave "Old Julia" and her grandchildren—John, Ham and Sarah—were believed to be with him. Dorcas was living in Haywood County, so in 1840, with the exception of five young slaves noted on the census, Robert was living alone.[168] An older slave does not appear there at that time. Curiously, two "free" female "colored persons" are enumerated in 1840 with Reuben Deaver in Buncombe County, one between the ages of ten and twenty-four, and another between the ages of thirty-six to fifty-five. Was the elder of them Julia? According to the 1850 and 1860 census records, she would have been sixty-five in 1840, at least a ten-year discrepancy. However, census records are not always accurate, so the possibility exists that the older "free" female in 1840 may have been Julia. If so, she was free long before the Civil War. Since slaves were moved back and forth quite often between Henry and Deaver, she may have been living at the springs for a time.

Julia was born in Africa about 1775. The birth of her son John is mentioned twice in Robert's personal notebook.[169] She built a home at the foot of a mountain owned by Henry, which became known as "Julia Knob" or "Julia Ridge." She cleared the land and lived there until her death. It is said that she would "shout and praise God when at work" and that her "disposition and character was so universally admired that a mountain was named after her."[170]

Julia is buried next to Robert in a small Clay County cemetery. A metal marker at Robert's grave, now missing, once read:

> *Born 10 Feb 1765, Died 1863. Julia: A slave belonging to Robert Henry, buried next to him. She would not take her freedom when it was given to her. She stayed to serve Robert Henry. Julia was known in the Tusquittee area for her good Christian character.*[171]

After ten years in Cherokee country, Robert was joined by his daughter Eliza, her children and her first husband, William G. Tidwell. The Tidwells had lived in South Carolina for several years, and their first child was born there in 1837. In 1845, their last child was born in Haywood County, North Carolina. But by 1847, William Tidwell was no longer living with his family. Eliza and her young children had taken residence at the home of her father.

Eliza divorced Tidwell sometime between 1847 and 1850. In January 1847, a legal announcement appeared in the *Highland Messenger* ordering Tidwell, who was out of state, to appear in Cherokee County court in March to answer her petition for divorce. If he failed to appear, a judgment would be rendered against him.

Eliza soon had a second husband, Narboone Moore, and in 1850, Robert Henry was counted on the census as living in their household. Sometime before 1858, apparently after the death of Moore, Eliza went west with Dr. C.N. Candler and was gone for about six months before returning. She left a second time and did not return. Eventually, she married Dr. Candler and lived in Arkansas, but without her children. In 1860, they were living in Robert Henry's home. Eliza "caused her family an ocean of trouble," stated Cornelia Henry.[172]

Back in Buncombe County, Reuben Deaver was tending to the Sulphur Springs operations. At first, it seemed to Robert that Reuben was a competent and able business partner. Yes, the pair had some disagreements, but the business was running smoothly enough, and Robert was content to stay in his new home.

However, once he and Deaver began having their differences and legal problems, Henry made several trips back to Buncombe County for the proceedings. In March 1851, after Robert received his summons to appear in Buncombe County court, he would spend much of the next nine years living in his home at Sulphur Springs.[173]

When Reuben Deaver died in 1852, his estate had insufficient assets to cover his debts. Robert's son William L. Henry became administrator of Reuben's estate after the death of Joshua Roberts, the first administrator. Over three hundred acres of Deaver's land were purchased by William at auction for $1,386.43 to cover Reuben's debt. The acreage included the Jarrett land, Deaver View and an 1833 land grant from the State of North Carolina.[174] Robert spent most of his time now at William's home.

More of Robert's family preceded him in death. In 1856, Robert learned that his grandson, Robert Pinckney Deaver, drowned in a shipwreck between Galveston and New Orleans. In 1857, ex-wife Dorcas Bell died after a long illness, and granddaughter Cora Henry died in 1858, not yet one year old. All were buried in the nearby Sulphur Springs Cemetery.

> *Dorcas B. Henry, late wife of Robert Henry, died in Asheville on Thursday the 5th day of February 1857.*

Robert was over ninety years old now, but he was still capable and competent enough to govern his business transactions and write out his own legal papers. Cornelia Henry remarked, "His mind is perfect yet, retains his memory well, though his eyesight is beginning to fail." He must have been troubled seeing his plantation deteriorating and slowly failing financially under his son's management. William was getting deeper and deeper into debt and was delinquent on many of his financial obligations. Robert may have had his disputes with Reuben Deaver, but his management abilities were certain to have been sorely missed. And now William was feuding with a man named C.C. Terry, the very person he had placed in the position of managing the hotel.

> [On] *Sunday & Monday, the 19th & 20th of Jan 1857, doves & other birds froze to death.*[175]

Robert began to dispose of some of his land. In 1855 and 1856, he sent William to the Western Country of Tennessee to locate and sell part of his holdings. On December 6, 1859, he sold 276 acres of his Tusquittee property to grandson William B. Tidwell. Three days later, he sold 770 acres of his Sulphur Springs Place to his son William for $1,600, subject to six notes totaling $10,000.[176]

On January 25, Robert wrote a new will. His Tidwell grandchildren had already been named as major recipients in an 1858 will, receiving slaves and thousands of acres of land. Now, in the 1860 revision, Martha Tidwell and Mary Tidwell Taylor were to receive thousands of dollars, which would be paid out of the money William L. Henry owed to his father. In addition, William B. Tidwell was named as one of the administrators of his estate. Although writing that his mind was "perfect," Cornelia Henry thought he had been under the influence of others. "I think it will take everything we have to pay the heirs of old Mr. Henry's estate," she wrote. "I wish he had kept it all & not been governed by William Tidwell."

Coincidentally (or perhaps not), William B. Tidwell had arrived at the Sulphur Springs Hotel on January 10, two weeks before Robert changed his will,[177] and Martha Tidwell was living there at the time. Shortly after, on March 2, "Old Mr. Tidwell" came to the hotel. He stayed until April 4, when he, Martha Tidwell and his other son, Robert Tidwell, left for home; Robert Tidwell to Henderson County, Tennessee, and he and Martha to Mississippi.[178]

On the morning of April 9, 1860, a very frail Robert Henry started to Cherokee on his final journey home. Cornelia Henry felt she would never see her father-in-law again.[179] In August, when living at his western home with William B. and Thomas P. Tidwell, his real estate was valued at $30,000, and he had a personal estate of $12,000.

In mid-March 1861, after the Sulphur Springs Hotel burned to the ground, creditors who were already waiting for William to pay his bills doubted his ability to do so even more. They began to file suit in court for payment of notes totaling nearly $6,000.[180] In August, William and Cornelia Henry visited Robert in Clay County. They could not have been bringing much, if any, good news. Cornelia wrote that they "went to Mr. Henry's father's. We traveled over some awful roads on Tusquittee Mountain. The scenery is grand on Nantahala, truly sublime. I enjoyed it finely. It was dark when we got to Papa's." While there, Robert was reflective, giving them a variation on the lyrics of an old seventeenth-century song. Cornelia wrote, "26th January 1862, Sunday, a beautiful day—These lines were given to us by our father, R. Henry, on last August. He was in his 95th year. He was born the 10th [of] Jan. 1767."[181]

One Hundred Years Hence[182]

Let us drink & be merry, dance, joke & rejoice,
With Claret canary & echoing voice.
This changeable world to our joys is unjust,
All pleasures are ended when we are in dust.
So in mirth let us spend our spare hours & pence,
For all shall be in pot one hundred years hence.

The beautiful damsel with garlands so crowned,
She kills with each glance as she treads on the ground.
Her glittering dress doth cast such a splendour,
Like nothing was fit but the stars to attend her.
Although she is pleasant & sweet to the sence,
She will be cold & mouldy one hundred years hence.

The greedy old miser gains hundreds of twentys,
And stares on his riches & pines among plenty.
He lays up great treasures he never will see,
The year of two thousand nine hundred & three.
He will leave all his savings his lands & his rents,
For a worm-eaten coffin one hundred years hence.

The true-hearted soldier a stranger to fear,
Calls up his spirits when danger is near.
He labors & fights great honors to gain,
Not doubting but that he will ever remain.

His courage and valour is of vain pretence,
For to flourish his standard one hundred years hence.

The merchant who ventures his all on the main,
Not doubting to grasp what the Indias contain.
He hussels & bussels like a bee in the spring,
Not knowing what harvest or autumn will bring.
Although fortunes great gain may lead him with pence,
He will ne'er reach the market one hundred years hence.

The plush coated Dr. his fees to enlarge,
Kills people by license & at their own charge.
He lays up great treasures of ill-gotten wealth,
The drugs of his pots the ruins of health.
The pleasures of health he pretends to dispence,
He will be turned into mummy one hundred years hence.

The rich brawling lawyer with fool wrangling strife,
Will plead you a tune to the end of your life.
He will plead you a tune while the client's in slavery,
The pleader makes conscience a cloak for his knavery.
He boasts of his cunning & brags of his sence,
He will be non est investrist one hundred years hence.

The priest tells that heaven is a happy place to dwell,
Compared with the pains & torments of hell.
He lives on the tithes of other men's labor,
And thinks that his blessings are viewed as a favor.
He talks of the spirits & bewilders the sence,
Knows not what will become of us one hundred years hence.

Why do we time all our trifles with cares,
Converting all our joys in sighs & to tears?
While pleasure abounds let us ever be tasting,
And drive away sorrow while vigour is lasting.
Let us kiss the brisk damsel that we may from thence,
Have heirs to succeed us one hundred years hence.

William L. Henry, son of Robert Henry, with his wife, Cornelia. *Courtesy of Don Taylor.*

In August 1862, Cornelia Henry received a report on Robert's health stating that, "Old Mr. Henry tolerable stout," but within six months, Robert was dead. On February 6, 1863, he died at his home in Clay County.[183] He was buried within one hundred yards of Compass Creek; his slave Julia was buried nearby. A headstone, erected by the Edward Buncombe Chapter of the Daughters of the American Revolution, reads, "Pioneer, Surveyor, Lawyer, Physician. He was also the first school master of Buncombe County and undoubtedly the last of the heroes of Kings Mountain."

Robert Henry reportedly had the gift of "sight" and therefore was able to predict the exact time of his death, as well as others, according to grandson Edmond L. (E.L.) Henry. Three times he had seen the "belled buzzard," a signal of impending death: twice for his sons, and once for himself. E.L., at the age of ten, went to visit his "grandsire" living in Tusquittee in Clay County.[184] One day during his visit, he went to see his cousin George Marstellar, who was living about four miles away. Robert Henry had been asked by Marstellar if he could borrow some of his slaves, as he had done quite often. E.L. relayed Robert Henry's reply to his cousin, saying, "Grandsire said for me to come and tell you that you cannot have one of his Negroes tomorrow because he will die at two o'clock today, and they will be busy burying him."

Edmond L. Henry (grandson of Robert Henry), Bell Taylor Plemondon and James Taylor at Robert Henry's grave. *Courtesy of Don Taylor.*

Above: James Taylor with daughter Bell Taylor Plemondon at Robert Henry's grave. *Courtesy of Don Taylor.*

Right: Robert Henry's headstone reads, "Robert Henry Born April 1765, Died 6 Feby 1863, Pioneer, Surveyor, Lawyer, Physician. He was also the first school master of Buncombe Co. and undoubtedly the last of the heroes of Kings Mountain." *Photo by author.*

Marstellar expressed disbelief and accompanied E.L. back to the Henry home. When they returned, Henry repeated his reason, ate a hearty dinner, talked for a while and lay down on a bearskin spread on the floor, as was his usual custom. When two o'clock arrived, his granddaughter Martha Tidwell, who was also there, remarked that he was still alive. Robert then directed his family to stretch out his body, and in a moment, he was dead.

This grand tale was labeled a "total fabrication" by William Vance Henry, a nephew of E.L. Henry. In fact, E.L. Henry, the source of the story, was born in 1865, two years after the death of his grandfather. When asked about the yarn years later, E.L. replied that yes, it was a fabrication, but it sure was a "good story."[185]

In more recent years, the figure of Robert Henry is said to have been seen by local residents near his grave dressed in colonial garb, sitting on the stump of an ancient tree, his eyes gazing over the beauty of his Carolina mountain paradise.

Chapter 13

Aftermath

The claim Robert M. Henry holds against me is fraudulent and injust.

Even after death, the patriarch of the Henry family managed to control his business affairs in minute detail. His final will—and a previous version of the same—spelled out all divestitures and the rationale for each. Not all disbursements were pleasant or agreeable to his heirs. While partial and generous to his grandchildren, others received nothing, creating conflicts that were left unresolved for many years.[186]

The deed to the Sulphur Springs property, including a gift of the house and furniture, was affirmed to William L. Henry, "subject only to the payment of the six notes which he owed me amounting in the whole to ten thousand dollars." Due to provisions in the will, William was now obligated to pay large portions of the $10,000 in notes to sisters Mary Taylor and Martha A. Arthur and niece Martha A. Tidwell.

Executor of Robert's estate was his grandson William B. Tidwell, the son of Eliza Henry and her first husband, William G. Tidwell. Robert lived with Eliza and her children for many years in Cherokee County, and for a time in 1860, he and granddaughter Martha Tidwell lived with William and Cornelia Henry in their Sulphur Springs home.

Eliza's children were well provided for, but Eliza received nothing from her father. In 1858, Robert explained:

> *Daughter Eliza made her elopement to the west with Doctor C.N. Candler and remained absent about six months and returned home. After her return,*

> *the subscriber believing that she had been cured of her vengeance, enquired of her if she was satisfied with the provisions made for her in my second will. She replied that she did not want me to will her anything but to divide it among her children, that she would live with them. Since that time, she has again eloped with the same Doctor C.N. Candler, and I expect she will never return. I need not state the character of Doctor Candler. It is known in Buncombe and Asheville.*

Eliza's son William B. Tidwell received two tracts of land in Cherokee County of about 276 acres, while Robert S. Tidwell gained approximately 2,000 acres in Henderson County, Tennessee, and more than 700 in Cherokee County. Thomas P. Tidwell was recipient of 50 acres on James Creek and part of a tract of land in Macon County known as the Big Glade.

Granddaughter Mary Tidwell had married a man named Newton Taylor. When Robert Henry did not approve of someone, he stated so, and he was not fond of Taylor. Newton apparently was not able to provide for his family. Mary Taylor, referred to as a "strange creature" by Cornelia Henry, appeared one day in 1860 at her door, "having to leave home for want of necessarys of life." The Taylors, she added, "have never treated me with any kindred feeling."

Thanks to his wife's family, Newton did find work a year later, when he was hired to work on the Henry mill dam and moved into one of the cabins on the nearby hill. Robert's opinion did not change, however, and since he had no confidence in Taylor, Mary's inheritance was placed in trust of her brother, William B. Tidwell. Mary was bequeathed a tract of land in Macon County of 105 acres, as well as about 400 acres in Cherokee County. A note of $2,500 was to be paid to her by W.L. Henry and placed in a trust for her or her sole descendants, and it was in "no event subject to the control or use of her said husband."

In addition to land and other assets, there was more "property" subject to be distributed. The slaves would have to be divided amongst the descendants. In 1858, Robert matter-of-factly explained how and why he would make his decisions:

> *In pursuance of the request of my daughter (Eliza) and my own will, I bequeath the following Negroes to her family, as I consider that they are entitled to them, for I offered to my daughter Polly on her marriage to Reuben Deaver a negro woman called Malinda. She refused to take her, alleging that she was of no account, that she would take money in*

> *her place. I then gave Malinda to my daughter Eliza. The negro woman had the following children, to wit: Catherine, Hamilton, Sarah, Tusquette, Sam, John sometimes called Tobi and Eliza. My daughter Eliza raised these children.*
>
> *William L. Henry sold Catherine to John Park, and my daughter Eliza was not benefitted by the sale. I therefore placed Negro John in her room, being nearly of the same age, and I sold Malinda, and Eliza was not benefitted by that sale. I therefore put Negro Mary, John's wife, in her place. In the different marriages of my daughter Eliza, I retained the right of these negroes knowing and believing that her different husbands are spendthrifts being part of their faults.*
>
> *The reason I have given the history of these negros is this. I give to my daughter Martha Arthur, upon her marriage, a negro woman then considered to be worth much more than the aforementioned negro Malinda, without reserving the title in myself, as I did with my daughter Eliza. Now the woman I give to my daughter Martha has not been as prolific as Malinda, and putting John in the place of Catharine, and his wife in the place of Malinda and their increase to the children of my daughter Eliza, it might be thought was too partial in favor of Eliza's children.*

William Henry received Sam (Buncombe Sam); his wife, Tena; and her four children: Athenly (Athaline), Charles, Haynes and Alonso. William B. Tidwell received slave John and his wife, Mary, and any children she may have. Thomas P. Tidwell received slaves Hamilton, Tusquitta, Sam and Eliza and any children that she may have. Mary Taylor received Sarah and child and any children she may have, and Martha A. Tidwell received slave John (sometimes called Tobe).

The remainder of the estate, real and personal, was given to daughter Martha Arthur and grandchildren Martha A. Tidwell and William B. Tidwell (in trust for Mary Taylor). Another grandson, William H. Deaver, was forgiven notes of $2,500 he owed Robert.

Conspicuous in their absence were Robert's sons James L. and Robert M. Henry. James had been the largest begatee of his mother's estate, of which Robert approved, so he received no more. Robert M. had also received much from his mother's estate. For that reason, and because Robert "had to pay on his account about three thousand dollars" and "his manner of life is well known," Robert M. received nothing.

In February 1864, Robert M. Henry, perhaps resentful of his exclusion, filed a lawsuit in the Court of Equity in Buncombe County. He stated that there had been a September 6, 1850 agreement between himself and William L. Henry to equally divide any property that may be willed in the future by their father:

> *Any property real or personal that may be acquired from either of their parents, either in the name of one or both of them, shall be held jointly between them, and if the conveyance is made in the name of one, he is to convey an equal interest in common to the other at a convenient, suitable and reasonable time; the said are to answer equally for all improvements put on any of their joint property, and if one or the other shall superintend the improvements of property, he shall be paid for it out of the property, making due allowance, etc., or otherwise paid.*

The agreement was made when the elder Robert Henry was contemplating the need for and had executed a will to divide his property between his children. It was to remain in force "as long as either of the parties to it shall wish it to continue, or until its being settled, at which time their joint property shall be divided between them."

Robert M. said that William was concerned that he was to receive fewer assets, so with a view of "perfect harmony," he offered William the agreement and boasted that their parents approved of the "good arrangement." Since then, though, he had been frequently absent while engaged in his profession, and William lived with their father most of the time until his death, exercising great control over his mind and inducing him to give William large sums of money, valuable negroes and land. Robert M. said his brother had purchased many tracts of land with their father's money. He charged William with prejudicing their father in order to get all the springs property, with his ultimate goal being to secretly dispose of it and leave the country. He believed that after William had purchased the hotel, he leased it to improvident and insolvent persons, mismanaged it and allowed it to decay. He had placed the property in the hands of an irresponsible man and through his and William's neglect, the hotel and furniture were consumed by fire. If he wasn't insolvent already, he concluded he would be soon.

Robert M. was not aware of the contents of Robert Henry's will, he said, because he was in the army of the Confederate States when his father died and did not return until September. After learning of them, he was ready to execute the agreement, but William refused.

William denied the accusations, filing his answer in the spring term of 1866, calling them fraudulent and countering with allegations of his own.

He charged his brother with trying to impeach their father's will and enlisting others to join him in the scheme. He would never have signed such an agreement as the one dated 1850 because it was always understood in the family, since his earliest recollection, that his father "denied that complainant was his child." Yes, the signature appeared to be his, he said, but he regularly signed blank documents for business purposes, leaving them with his brother, and if he signed anything, the top must have been blank and filled in with the agreement. William charged that Robert M. was a drunkard, stating that he was forced to pay his bills many times, as well as feed him and his horse repeatedly. He would "attend to nothing, kept drunk and would gamble away and waste all the money that he could get hold of."

Any money he spent of his father's or received from his father, William explained, was accounted for. Large sums received from land sales in Tennessee were used under his father's direction to pay his father's liabilities. Also, much of it was used to pay claims filed against his brother.

In an undated and unsigned letter appearing to be in William's handwriting, he states the worst day's work he ever did was in the spring of 1853, when under the influence of his mother and Robert M., he took his brother in as a partner. At that point, they agreed to keep the Sulphur Springs Hotel jointly, but nothing else. This was the only contract he ever signed, and it was witnessed by his sister Eliza. He was to be reimbursed from the proceeds for all his previous outlays supporting Robert M., which he listed as several thousand dollars. After making any necessary repairs, net profits and losses were to be divided equally. But, he said, Robert M. attended closely to the bar and always left an empty till. In describing his brother's legal practice, he noted his frequent customers were a certain kind of "red monkeys only seen by professional practitioners of his order and degree in the arts."

When William feared he may not return home from a local Civil War skirmish, he entered a will and statement in his wife's daily journal:

> *4th February 1865—As the enemy are reported to be on Johnathan's Creek and I am going with the command to meet them, I will only say that all or any of my property that may be left after paying my just debts, I want my wife Cornelia Catherine to have and to hold and dispose of to suit herself either by sale or gift.*
>
> *The claim Robert M. Henry holds against me is fraudulent and injust & I have employed my old friend Mr. N.W. Woodfin & Judge Baily as atternies & I wish every evidence searched for. Sister Eliza was a witness in all the agreement I ever had with Robt. M. H. & that was about keeping*

> *the hotel & settlement was demanded on all and everything outstanding between us in the year of 1855. The witness G.W. Peake was present & J.L. Henry knows we quit all business together.*[187]

In the fall term of 1866, Robert M. filed exceptions to several of William's answers, labeling them "irrelevant, scandalous and impertinent." The judge agreed, so William appealed to the North Carolina Supreme Court. In January 1868, the court allowed the accusatory and inflammatory language of his initial reply, stating that, "Although they are abusive and disparaging, they are not impertinent, but are relevant." William may have had some hope when another trial was ordered by the court.

Then, sometime after 1863, the original will of Robert Henry disappeared. A petition was filed in Buncombe County Superior Court in February 1870 to "establish Last Will and Testament of Robert Henry" by the estate administrator, Samuel Gudger. The petition stated that the will had been proved in court and ordered to be recorded but was either lost or abstracted from the office of the clerk of the court before recorded, or "if recorded at all, the record thereof had also been burnt, obliterated or destroyed so that no trace of the original will or the record thereof can now be found." Whether the will was purposely removed or was consumed by an 1865 courthouse fire is unknown.

A duplicate of the will was produced in court by the petitioners that "was taken and preserved before the loss of the original." The petition was not contested, so the court found the copy valid.[188]

In the meantime, William Henry's financial woes were escalating. He was going broke, just as his brother had predicted. The hotel had burned to the ground, and because of the war, he no longer had access to slave labor. He still owed the payments stipulated in Robert's will, as well as many other debts. Cornelia Henry wrote:

> *September 1865, Monday 25th—Mr. Henry went to town. He has the blues…for fear his debts will break him up. I hope not. He will hate to give up his homestead and mills and everything he has.*
>
> *November 4th, 1865—The war has broken us up. I can't see how we are to pay our debts & still retain a home. Mr. Henry worries about it a good deal. He is prematurely ten years older in the last eight months. The loss of the hotel hurt him a great deal and now the negroes being freed is another blow.*

January 1867, Saturday 12th—As we are so poor, I am not able to buy a little crewel to work with. What is to become of us I don't know. I think it will take everything we have to pay the heirs of old Mr. Henry's estate.[189]

Although he continued to operate his mills, farm and wagon shop, William struggled financially. At some point, he had invested in the Jones Gap Turnpike Company and the Little River Turnpike. Ownership of a turnpike certificate was considered a valuable possession and generally provided some good income.[190] He worked maintenance on the road and set up his own tollgate, but in April 1869, the General Assembly of North Carolina ratified an act that disallowed the gate, naming William specifically. Now that income was gone, too.

Court judgments for non-payment began to accumulate. On July 1, 1871, William was forced to sell land at a sheriff's sale to pay creditors. Parcels were purchased by W.W. Rollins, Pinckney Rollins, G.M. Roberts and William's brother James L. Henry.

At the 1869 spring term of the Superior Court of Buncombe County, the "Rollins group," now representing William's interests as their own, and R.M. Henry agreed to defer the case to J.G. Martin and W.D. Rankin as referees. Their decision would be regarded as a rule of the court. In the 1872 fall term, they ruled that the 1850 agreement between William and Robert M. was indeed genuine, binding and applicable to the Sulphur Springs property and that the property should be divided equally between them.

Both parties filed exceptions, and by the spring term of 1873, the case had been pended and moved from court to court. Another year later, on March 14, 1874, the Graham County court ruled in favor of Robert M. Henry and awarded him deeds to several of William's properties. He would recover not only the original Sulphur Springs tract purchased by Robert Henry but also many other tracts, including those William had purchased from Reuben Deaver's estate. William was ordered to execute a deed of conveyance totaling over one thousand acres to his brother.

The court case appeared closed, but the final execution of Robert Henry's estate had not yet been resolved. In July 1872, the Haywood County court ruled Robert's estate owed more than $6,000. In September, William was forced to sell more of his land at public auction to pay the debt. Again, the purchasers were the Rollins group and J.L. Henry. J.L. transferred his interests to the other parties in 1874. The Rollins group was well aware of the other legal disputes and agreed to defend the interests of William Henry for their own benefit.

W.W. Rollins, Pinckney Rollins and another partner, L.M. Welch, now claimed title to Robert Henry's lands, as they believed they had legally purchased them from William at two sheriff's sales. In September 1874, they petitioned the court asking that the earlier Graham County decree in favor of Robert M. Henry be set aside and that he be restrained from taking possession. They were successful in receiving the restraining order, but after another series of back-and-forth court rulings, they transferred their interest in a portion of the property to the Falls of Neuse Manufacturing Company.

Because the titles had been awarded by the Superior Court of Graham County to Robert M. Henry in 1874, William finally deeded them to him on January 30, 1876, as the court had ordered. W.W. Rollins and his partners sold their remaining springs land to the Falls of Neuse Manufacturing Company. To do so, they had to clear the legal title, so Rollins filed a "Civil Action to Recover The Sulphur Springs Land" at the 1877 fall term of Buncombe Superior Court.[191]

Both the Rollins group and R.M. Henry were now claiming ownership through W.L. Henry; the Rollins group through the sheriff's sales, and R.M. Henry through the decision of the court and the transfer of titles from William in 1876. In the January 1878 term of the North Carolina Supreme Court, the Rollins group argued that any decree transferring the title of the Sulphur Springs land to R.M. Henry under the 1850 agreement should have been considered fraudulent. Evidence supporting their argument was submitted to the jury, which agreed and found that the Rollins group, not Robert M. Henry, was the true owner and entitled to recover damages. The Graham County court verdict was fraudulent because it gave Robert M. a greater estate in the property than he was equitably entitled. Although the agreement itself between the brothers was valid, it applied only to lands given or willed by the elder Henry and not to those legally sold.

Finally, in 1881, after seventeen years of legal battles, the Supreme Court upheld the decision. The 1850 agreement was "confined to property acquired by gift, will or inheritance." The land had indeed belonged to William L. Henry and then the Rollins group, which was additionally entitled to damages of $600 for each of the four years of Robert M. Henry's occupation.

The Falls of Neuse Manufacturing Company was now owner of the Sulphur Springs land. In 1886, it sold sixty-one acres, known as the "Hotel Tract," to Thomas Van Gilder and Edwin G. Carrier. Carrier built his new brick hotel on the same site as Henry and Deaver's first wooden structure.

The remaining Henry plantation was reduced to a small number of acres surrounding the Henry Mills on Hominy Creek. In 1890, the small farm was ruled a homestead and excepted from any sale under execution. William Henry's home and property were valued at $1,500. His remaining personal property was two horses, three cows and calves, two yearlings, fifteen hogs, thirty-five sheep, one bull, some household and kitchen furniture, farming tools and a wagon.[192]

Epilogue

Nearly 250 years have passed since the birth of Robert Henry, a truly remarkable man who is now virtually forgotten and unknown within the very community in which he was so successful. There are many factors that may have contributed to this anonymity.

Robert was an eccentric man, spending his later years in western North Carolina, far removed from the Sulphur Springs. He lived a quiet life near Tusquittee Creek while tending to his farm. Surviving well into his nineties, he outlived his contemporaries who would have known and remembered him after he left Buncombe County. He is buried in a remote area of Clay County where few will see his grave.

Robert could be unbearable when intoxicated—and probably at times when he was sober. He appears to have had a low tolerance for the opinions of others, giving them little credence, and spoke his mind matter-of-factly, regardless of the consequences. Mistreated family members and relatives would not have remembered him in a positive light.

Following his death, the loss of the hotel, the after effects of the Civil War and prolonged legal battles, his son William incurred huge debts, suffered lawsuits and eventually sold or lost hundreds of acres of Robert Henry's estate. In addition, little physical evidence remains of the Henry homestead or large plantation. Only a small road sign commemorates the existence of the historic Sulphur Springs resort. Henry's orchards, gardens and pastures have disappeared and are now covered by streets, houses, sidewalks and well-manicured lawns. The meadow is a lonesome, overgrown valley within which the Caney Creek branch flows. The Sulphur Springs Academy that stood next the cemetery was torn down sometime after the Civil War.

Every day, vehicles cross the Bear Creek Road bridge over Hominy Creek, their occupants unaware that, in reality, the "creek" was dug by slaves and was the race for the mill dam; that in Revolutionary days, North Carolina militiamen had camped in close proximity; or that the centuries-old "Township Tree" still stands on a nearby hill. Small remnants of the dams now appear as ripples in the water or flat stones stacked on the bank, visible only to those who know where to look.

The more modern resort hotel built in the latter part of the 1880s burned to the ground. The Malvern Hills clubhouse and golf course disappeared long ago, except for a vine-enveloped octagonal pavilion over the spring, which has ceased to flow, and piles of broken and crumbled bricks. The

Pencil sketch believed to be Robert Henry, circa 1840. *Henry Archive (private collection).*

park once encompassing the Sulphur Springs has reverted back to a wild, unkempt state.

We must strive to uncover, preserve and remember our forgotten local history and those who played a role in its creation. Much of that history in western North Carolina is forever tied to Robert Henry. Very few men could claim to have lived such a versatile life. Henry's influence in the community no doubt had a major impact on the future of Asheville and was certainly a catalyst for early mountain tourism and development.

Robert began his life in a wild, new country where men carved out the existence of their choosing. He witnessed events that shaped the beginning of a free nation and then fought to secure that freedom. He became a lawyer, surveyor, landowner and speculator, businessman and entrepreneur. He surveyed state boundary lines and the lands of a native people who would be forced from their homes. He was alive at the time of the War of 1812 and half a century later saw North Carolina secede from the country for which he had fought so bravely.

In March 1928, the *Asheville Citizen* published historian F.A. Sondley's rambling biography of Robert Henry as a special series, receiving attention throughout western North Carolina and beyond. The *Clay County News* suggested that a day be set aside in the summer and established as a tribute to this forgotten citizen.[193] Word of a possible monument honoring Henry reached sculptor Duane Champlain in New York City. Champlain offered to construct a scale model of the grounds to exhibit as an example and to generate more interest.[194] When a new bridge was built spanning the French Broad River, it was suggested it should be named after Henry.[195] Unfortunately, none of these suggestions came to fruition. Perhaps it is still not too late to "let honor be given to whom honor is due."

Notes

1. *Clay County News*, March 7, 1928.

Introduction

2. Browder, "The Cherokee Indians." Browder claims that many of Robert's exploits may have been total fabrication. Most historians, however, consider his accounts as generally trustworthy and believable. In addition, John Preston Arthur, F.A. Sondley and Lyman C. Draper relied heavily on information provided by Robert Henry and his descendants. Incidents known to be myth or invention have been identified and described as such within this work.

Chapter 1

3. James Henry, "Henry Family History."
4. Sondley, "Robert Henry Biography." Statements regarding Henry family history not documented from a specific primary source are referenced from Robert Henry's personal notebooks and several written histories, including Arthur (1914), F.A. Sondley (1928), T.P. Tidwell (1991) and J.T. Henry (1947). F.A. Sondley was a contemporary with Henry descendants. John Preston Arthur, Thomas P. Tidwell and James T. Henry were grandsons of Robert Henry.
5. James Henry, "Henry Family History." Another researcher (E.D. Tidwell) asserts that Thomas arrived in Augusta County, Virginia, in 1733 at age fourteen with brothers Malcolm and William and then came to North

Carolina in 1744. If so, Thomas was likely not yet a carpenter, married or of sufficient age to have been a veteran of the British military.

6. Sondley, "Robert Henry Biography."
7. Letter from Kathy Nebel to Charlotte-Mecklenburg Parks and Recreation Committee, July 24, 2000. Information from Charlotte-Mecklenburg Historic Landmarks Commission, historic landmark designation application for the Tuckasegee Ford and Trail.
8. Carter, *Pioneer Houses and Homesteads*.
9. Holcomb, *Deed Abstracts of Mecklenburg County*; Puett, *The History of Gaston County*.
10. Robert Henry, "Personal Notebook."
11. Sondley, "Robert Henry Biography"; *Pruitt, Abstracts of Land Entries: Buncombe Co., NC*. A land grant filing in September 1786 may support 1765 as the year of birth for Robert Henry, as he would have been twenty-one years of age. If born in 1767, he would have been only nineteen.
12. Ragan, *The History of Gastonia*; Puett, *The History of Gaston County*.
13. The 1880 census records of Joseph's sons Noah Henry of Henderson County, North Carolina, and Ephraim Henry of Rock Prairie, Missouri, both indicate that Joseph was born in North Carolina.
14. Sondley gives the name Martha Shields. E.D. Tidwell states that Isabella was born about 1720 as Martha Isabella Shields.
15. Holcomb, *Deed Abstracts of Mecklenburg County*.
16. Beatty, "Will of Francis Beatty."
17. According to his headstone inscription and Robert Henry's notebook.
18. North Carolina, Estate Files, 1663–1979, *FamilySearch*, https://familysearch.org/pal:/MM9.1.1/VH6X-RG5, Thomas Henry, 1791.
19. Sondley's source was Robert Henry's grandson Edmond L. Henry.
20. Tidwell and Tidwell, *Tidwell and Etherton Family*; James Henry, "Henry Family History"; "Robert Henry, Personal Notebook." Also, male heirs were noted in a September 18, 1800 Lincoln County deed (see Pruitt, *Abstracts of Lincolnton, NC Deeds*) and in a slave relinquishment document dated November 28, 1837 (North Carolina Collection, Pack Library, Asheville, NC).
21. January 9, 1767, is the date of birth Robert Henry entered in his notebook. Cornelia Henry quoted the same date in *Fear in North Carolina*. After interviewing Robert Henry on September 29, 1858, Robert C. Gillam wrote that regarding the Battle of Kings Mountain, "He [Robert] says that he was thirteen years of age." From the journal of Cornelia Henry, an entry by William L. Henry states, "My father was borned on the 10 Jany 1767. Consequently, he is now 94 years old."

22. Cornelia Henry, *Fear in North Carolina*. Cornelia Henry states that Robert Henry died sometime in January 1863. Different handwriting (not Robert's or Cornelia's) in Robert Henry's notebook gives February 6, 1863, as his date of death.

Chapter 2

23. Baer, *The Natural History of Rabies*.
24. Sondley, "Robert Henry Biography"; Schenck, *Diary of David Schenck*. In his September 12, 1859 diary entry, Schenck writes that the information regarding the Mecklenburg Declaration was given to him by Colonel Moses Henry, a cousin of Robert Henry who had recently visited him at Deaver's Springs.
25. Schenck, "Letter to the Editor."
26. Ibid.; Schenck, *Diary of David Schenck*, 151–52.
27. Schenck, "Letter to the Editor"; Sondley, "Robert Henry Biography."
28. Davidson, *Reminiscences in the Lyceum*.

Chapter 3

29. Anderson, *Lincoln County Men*.
30. Bell, "List of Names in Christian Carpenter's Army."
31. Dameron, *Kings Mountain*, 27.
32. W.L. Henry, "Unsigned Letter."
33. On December 21, 1780, Brigadier General Daniel Morgan left Charlotte, North Carolina, in command of six hundred light infantry. He traveled west to take position between the Broad and Pacolet Rivers to protect the locals. By Christmas Day, when Morgan had reached the Pacolet, he was joined by other militia from Georgia and the Carolinas. He camped there until January 16, when he began a march to Cowpens. Thomas may have joined when Morgan headed out of Charlotte, or he may have already been in South Carolina and joined Morgan when the other militia from Georgia and the Carolinas joined Morgan's camp.
34. Tryon County was divided into Lincoln and Rutherford Counties in April 1799.
35. Dameron, *Kings Mountain*, 30.
36. Vance, *Narrative of the Battle of Kings Mountain*.
37. Gudger, "Early Historic Manuscript of Buncombe County."
38. Vance, *Narrative of the Battle of Kings Mountain*.

39. Logan, "Robert C. Gilliam to Dr. J.H. Logan."
40. Henry's quotes are taken from his Kings Mountain account in *Narrative of the Battle of Kings Mountain*, by David Vance.
41. Logan, "Robert C. Gilliam to Dr. J.H. Logan."
42. Ibid.
43. Origins of the phrase "blue hen's chickens" vary, although in this instance, it could have originated as related in the following 1856 anecdote from Oliver Bunce's *The Romance of the Revolution* (page 361):

> *Revolutionary War General Thomas Sumter, while seeking recruits for the war, encountered several brothers named Gillespie. The Gillespies possessed a blue hen "of the fighting species," the offspring of which were known for their courage in the sport of cock-fighting. Sumter, appearing suddenly during the match, disgustedly told the brothers of the cruelty of their game. He said if they went with him, he would give them a worthier game and "teach them how to fight with men." Believing his words, the boys yelled their ultimate compliment: "He is one of the Blue Hen's chickens!" and he became known as the Gamecock.*

Robert Henry was quoted in the November, 8 1859 issue of the *Western Democrat* as stating that a Gilmore, not a Gillespie, had owned a fighting chicken named Tuck and that that was Sumter's first nickname.

Chapter 4

44. "The movements of Colonel Locke and his men for the months following were confined to his immediate section until the spring of 1781." McCorkle, "Sketch of Colonel Francis Locke"; Joseph Henry, "Revolutionary War Pension Application of Joseph Henry."
45. Joseph Henry, "Revolutionary War Pension Application of Joseph Henry"; Robert Henry, "Narrative of the Battle of Cowan's Ford." Joseph Henry was drafted for a second tour in December 1780 under the command of Colonel Frances Locke in Captain Loftin's company. He marched through Lincoln, Mecklenburg, Rowan and Guilford Counties. He was finally discharged on the Haw River in Guilford County and never participated in any engagement. His term of service ended on March 3, 1781, before the Guilford Courthouse battle. The above timeline coincides with Joseph's warning at Beatty's school before the Battle of Cowan's Ford.

46. Near present-day Belmont, North Carolina, on January 31, 1781.
47. James Henry, "Henry Family History"; Tidwell and Tidwell, *Tidwell and Etherton Family*.
48. William L. Henry, "Unsigned Letter"; Joseph Henry, "Revolutionary War Pension Application of Joseph Henry." Joseph Henry's second tour was under the command of Colonel Frances Locke in Captain Loftin's company. Loftin's pension application states that they fought at Cowan's Ford, but Joseph's pension application states that he was in no battles. Because Joseph left to warn others about the British, he may not have been at the ford. When Robert returned home, Joseph was there with Robert's other friends.
49. Graham, "The Battle at Cowan's Ford."
50. Buchanan, *The Road to Guilford Courthouse*, 429; Davidson, *Piedmont Partisan*.
51. Schenck is likely referring to his book *North Carolina, 1780–81: Being a History of the Invasion of the Carolinas* (1889).
52. Schenck, "Letter to the Compiler."

Chapter 5

53. Arthur, *Western North Carolina*, 406; Revolutionary War Pay Voucher #324, September 26,1781.
54. Tennent, *The Indian Path*.
55. Blount, "Letter to Robert Love, December 7, 1795" in *The John Gray Blount Papers*, 616.
56. Sondley, "Robert Henry Biography."
57. Sondley, *The Indian's Curse*. In Sondley's version of the tale, it was General Rutherford and his men who made camp on Hominy Creek, staying there for a week.
58. Gudger, "Early Historic Manuscript of Buncombe County"; Tennent, *The Indian Path*.
59. Manning, *Buncombe County Court Records*.
60. Blackmun, *Western North Carolina*, 163, 186.
61. Blackmun, *A Spire in the Mountains*, 14, 17.
62. Arthur, *Western North Carolina*, 424.
63. Sondley, *A History of Buncombe County*, 770.

Chapter 6

64. "An Act for Commissioners to Settle the Boundary Line between This State and the State of Tennessee, 1796." North Carolina Department of Archives and History.
65. Powell, *Dictionary of North Carolina Biography*.
66. Jane (Jean) Henry, Robert's sister, was mentioned in Francis Beatty's will as "the eldest daughter of my cousin Thomas Henry."
67. Bedini, *Early American Surveyors*, 35.
68. Much of the information provided here regarding the processes of surveying was obtained from Bedini's *Early American Surveyors* and *Thinkers and Tinkers*, Howard's *Recollections of Tennessee* and Mills's "Surveying in the Mountains of Western North Carolina."
69. Howard, *Recollections of Tennessee*.
70. Vance, *Narrative of the Battle of Kings Mountain*, statement of Robert Henry.
71. Arthur, *Western North Carolina*.
72. Strother, John Strother Diary.
73. Ibid.
74. Vance, *Narrative of the Battle of Kings Mountain*.
75. Strother, John Strother Diary.

Chapter 7

76. In April 1799, this portion of Tryon County became Lincoln County.
77. Statement of Elizabeth Henry Laisy.
78. Other remedies:

> *Cold or Catarrh—The following cure I discovered by accident. When a small boy, I was fond of raw onions, and my mother raised a number of them. She had gathered her crop of them, and I went into the garden and found occasion to eat as many of them as I wanted, and having a bad cold and severe cough discharging tough mucous or canker. On the next day, I observed my discharge was of a yellow consistency easily thrown off, and in a very short time, the cough ceased. I followed this remedy in future with effect. I afterwards discovered that garlic was more potent than onions and found that by taking pulverized sulphur at the time of taking the onion was such a help.*
>
> *Another cure, when a person is troubled with a cold or cough, that if he will take a drink of warm whiskey for a few times it will remove the cough. If you are troubled with sneezing and coughing, the incipient stage of a*

cold, sit with your back to a warm fire, and your sneezing will stop in a few minutes. Those who use onions, whether raw or cooked, are seldom troubled with the cold or a cough. If the foregoing remedies fail, then you may expect that the lungs are affected and a consumption has commenced. I have been this particular in giving various cures for the cold that are in every bodies power, for the cold will sometimes terminate in consumption, a disease when far advanced will be out of the reach of medicine.

79. Robert Henry, "Narrative of the Battle of Cowan's Ford." Ora Blackmon states that Robert left Union Hill to practice law, while F.A. Sondley indicates that he left to become a surveyor, studying law at a later date. A grandson, James T. Henry, stated that his grandfather studied law and medicine for three years in Columbia, South Carolina, before settling in Buncombe County.
80. Cope and Wellman, *The County of Gaston.*
81. Manning, *Buncombe County Court Records.*
82. Sondley, "Robert Henry Biography."
83. Davidson, *Reminisces in the Lyceum.*
84. Sondley, "Robert Henry Biography."
85. Brown, "John Preston Arthur."
86. Sondley, "Robert Henry Biography." Robert Love is said to have been the inspiration and model for the Indian fighter in Robert Strange's novel *Eoneguski.*
87. Strange, *Eoneguski.*
88. Sondley, "Robert Henry Biography."
89. Arthur, *Western North Carolina*, 381.
90. *Raleigh Register and North Carolina Weekly Advertiser*, November 22.
91. Haywood, *A Manual of Laws*, 104.
92. Manning, *Buncombe County Court Records*; Sondley, "Robert Henry Biography."
93. Manning, *Buncombe County Court Records.*
94. Arthur, *Western North Carolina*, 387.
95. *Western Carolinian*, March 23, 1824.
96. Sondley, "Robert Henry Biography."
97. Arthur, *Western North Carolina*; letter from William Tolliver (author's collection).
98. Arthur, *Western North Carolina.*
99. Wilkes County Superior Court Minutes, 1807–1820, March Term, 1811, CR 104.311.1.

Chapter 8

100. Pruitt, *Abstracts of Land Entries: Buncombe Co., NC.*
101. Hart, *American History*, 388.
102. Hunter, *Sketches of Western North Carolina.*
103. McLean, "Journey to Tennessee."
104. *Fayetteville Carolina Observer*, June 12, 1832.
105. Manning, *Buncombe County Court Records.*
106. Marsh and Marsh, *Early Unpublished Court Records of Lincoln County*; Manning, *Buncombe County Court Records.*
107. Manning, *Buncombe County Court Records.*
108. Love, "Letter." "Jonny is living with his brother-in-law, Robert Henry, reading law, and he is the clerk of the Superior Court of Haywood County."
109. Buncombe County Register of Deeds; Cornelia Henry, "February 1, 1860," in *Fear in North Carolina.*
110. Abernethy, *From Frontier to Plantation*, 53–54.
111. Pruitt, *Glasgow Land Fraud Papers.* On April 26, 1820, Joseph Dickson assigned 640 acres in Tennessee's tenth district to Robert Henry (Tennessee Revolutionary War Warrant 296, Grant 21490). On August 24, 1820, the heirs of Corporal Alexander Coles assigned 360 acres to Henry (Warrant 355). On September 22, 1820, Private Charles Williamson assigned 274 acres in the tenth district to Henry (Warrant 576). On May 7, 1821, James McKee, heir of Captain William Chronicle, assigned Henry 3,840 acres (Warrant 654, issued on November 23, 1820). On February 24, 1824, John Armstrong assigned 50 acres to Henry (grant 21494).
112. Robert Henry, "Instructions for William L. Henry."

Chapter 9

113. John Love, son of Robert Love, had read law with Henry in 1814.
114. *Raleigh Register*, January 10, 1823. Other appointees were Samuel Chunn, Samuel Davidson, Philip Britton, Benjamin King, Garet Duese and Zephania Horton. The November 25, 1823 edition of the *Western Carolinian* reported Philip Brittain as the only delegate from Buncombe County who attended the November 10–17, 1823 meeting of the committee in Raleigh.
115. Robert Henry, "Personal Notebook." Elizabeth's tombstone states 1822.
116. On a federal census dated August 7, 1820, Robert Henry was noted as living in Buncombe County next to Russell Jones.

117. Mary Gudger Moore was the wife of William H. Moore, the grandson of William Moore of the Indian campaign.
118. In this chapter, extensive reference is made to testimony from the Supreme Court of North Carolina case *Deaver v. Henry* and associated cases.
119. Possibly Alexander P. Henry, son of Robert's brother Joseph Henry. In later years, Jack was instructed in the carpenter's trade by a Captain Nichols, an employee of Reuben Deaver.
120. *Deaver v. Henry*.
121. *Annual Report of the American Bible Society*, 551.
122. *Charleston Courier*, August 10, 1845.
123. Robert Henry, "Personal Notebook."
124. Arthur, *Western North Carolina*.
125. Cornelia Henry, *Fear in North Carolina*.
126. Colton, *Mountain Scenery*.
127. *Charleston Mercury*, August 31, 1859.
128. Lanman, "Letters from the Allegheny Mountains."
129. John Harrington to Reverend W.M. Reid, July 4, 1837.
130. *Charleston Courier*, October 26, 1837.
131. Moore, "Some Early Recollections."
132. *Charleston Courier*, August 10, 1845.
133. Arthur, *Western North Carolina*, 502.
134. Blackmun, *Western North Carolina*.
135. McKeithen, "Sulphur Springs Letter."
136. Olmsted, *A Journey in the Back Country*, 261.
137. Cornelia Henry, *Fear in North Carolina*. Uncle Andy was a Henry family slave.
138. *Charleston Courier*, March 20, 1861.
139. *Charleston Mercury*, June 29, 1859.
140. Cornelia Henry, *Fear in North Carolina*.
141. Arthur, *Western North Carolina*.

Chapter 10

142. Agnes Mary Clerke, *A Popular History of Astronomy During the Nineteenth Century*. London: Adam and Charles Black, 1893.
143. Children of Robert and Dorcas Bell Henry were: Mary Louise "Polly" Henry (1815–1844), Elizabeth Isabella Henry (1818–1915), Robert Marcellus Henry (1821–1885), William Lewis Henry (1823–1900), Martha Ann Henry (1826–1896) and James Love Henry (1835–1884).

144. *Dorcas B. Henry v. Robert Henry.*
145. Greene, "A Struggle for Cherokee Community."
146. Haywood County Court Minutes, December 1834–January 1838.
147. Deaver, "Reuben Deaver to E.B. Dudley."
148. *Deaver v. Henry*. From the $112 William Henry earned as a chain bearer, he used $100 to purchase a mare from Reuben Deaver in 1839.
149. Moore, "Some Early Recollections."
150. Greene, "A Struggle for Cherokee Community."
151. Freel, *Our Heritage*.
152. Powell, *Dictionary of North Carolina Biography*.
153. *Deaver v. Henry*. Expenses for an 1838 journey to "The Nation" appear in Robert Henry's ledger.
154. Riggs and Greene, "The Cherokee Trail of Tears."
155. Ibid.; Greene, "A Struggle for Cherokee Community."
156. Spindel, *Introductory Guide*.
157. Julia and her grandson John were noted as being under the control of Reuben Deaver until 1844.
158. Deaver, "Field Book of Lands."
159. Arthur, *Western North Carolina*, 290.

Chapter 11

160. North Carolina, Haywood County, Superior Court of Law, 1842.
161. Extensive reference is made in this chapter to testimony from the Supreme Court of North Carolina case *Deaver v. Henry* and associated cases.
162. William Francis was called in to act as umpire in case of a voting deadlock.
163. Reuben Deaver married Mary S. Torian of Perquimans County, North Carolina, on April 26, 1847.
164. On December 8, 1841, Reuben Deaver received survey warrant 6550 for thirty-six acres on the west side of the French Broad River, including the building at Sulphur Springs. The grant was issued on January 10, 1843, for lands previously conveyed and in possession of Robert Henry that had been surveyed on November 12, 1842.
165. Testimony of James R. Love in *Deaver v. Henry*.

Chapter 12

166. Draper, *Kings Mountain and Its Heroes*, 259.
167. Other land transactions included Land Grant #2769 on September

22, 1838, in Clay and Cherokee County, and on the same date there is an entry for 400 acres in Macon County. On April 18, 1839, the State of North Carolina granted Robert Henry 165 acres on the French Broad River. On April 14, 1840, Robert entered for 6 acres next to Joseph Henry on the north side of the French Broad River in Henderson County; on April 15, 1840, he entered for another 100. On November 21, 1846, Robert Henry "of Cherokee County" (with W.L. Henry as his agent) sold 360 acres to Thomas M. Davis on the west side of the south fork of the Forked Deer River in Madison County, Tennessee.

168. Listed in the census were one male and one female slave under ten and three males aged ten to twenty-four.

169. Henry wrote, "Julia's child John was born 6th February 1823" and "Negro John was born the 6th day of February 1823." Slave schedules in 1850 and 1860 both enumerate an elderly female slave living on Robert's farm.

170. Freel, *Our Heritage*, 99; Sharpe, *A New Geography of North Carolina.*

171. Shepard, "Clay County, NC—Cemeteries."

172. Cornelia Henry, *Fear in North Carolina.*

173. Several sources indicate that Robert was living in Buncombe County: Robert Henry was to take depositions of witnesses in Deaver v, Henry on February 21, 22, and 23, 1853 at his dwelling near Sulphur Springs; Instructions for William L. Henry on locating papers for Robert Henry's land in the western district of Tennessee was sent from Sulphur Springs, May 11, 1856, Buncombe County, N.C.; A letter from William L. Henry to Cornelia Henry at Sulphur Springs, May 29, 1856, Fayetteville, Tennessee, states "say to Papa that the District land can be secured;" An article in the Western Democrat, November, 8 1859 states Robert Henry was residing at "Denver [Deaver's] Springs;" An entry in Cornelia Henry's Journal, January 8, 1860 states "I forgot to mention in the proper place that old Mr. Henry was living with us, also Martha Tidwell."

174. Buncombe County Deed Book 20, 280.

175. Kocin and Uccellini, *Snowstorms.* "The Cold Storm" of 1857 produced severe blizzard conditions and below-freezing temperatures from North Carolina to Maine.

176. Buncombe County Deed Book 27, 215–16, 364.

177. Cornelia Henry, *Fear in North Carolina.*

178. Ibid.

179. Ibid.

180. A February 11, 1861 note to J.F.E. Hardy for $916.00, an April 15, 1861 note to J.F.E. Hardy for $1,865.60 and a note to Goran Mills for $3,000.00.
181. Cornelia Henry, *Fear in North Carolina.*
182. In *The Triumphs of London* (1675), Thomas Jordan called the song *The Epicure: Sung By One in the Habit of a Town Gallant.* It also appeared in the songbook Choice Ayres, Songs & Dialogues, I, 1675, set to a Robert Smith tune that had been used for *The Longing Maid.* See Claude M. Simpson, *The British Broadside Ballad and Its Music.* New Brunswick, NJ: Rutgers University Press, 1966.
183. Cornelia Henry, *Fear in North Carolina.* "Old Mr. Henry died some time in Jan. 1863."
184. Sondley, "Robert Henry Biography."
185. Elizabeth Henry Laisy as recorded by William Vance Henry.

Chapter 13

186. Two Robert Henry wills are known to exist. The first, dated 1858 and located in the North Carolina Archives, gives explanations of many of Robert's decisions. The second, dated 1860, is the will approved as the legal document by the Buncombe County court.
187. Cornelia Henry, *Fear in North Carolina.*
188. An examination of this will and one dated 1858 reveals that they are essentially the same document.
189. Cornelia Henry, *Fear in North Carolina.*
190. *Brevard News,* January 11, 1929.
191. *W.W. Rollins and Others v. R.M. Henry and Others.*
192. Buncombe County Register of Deeds, Book 69, 330–31.

Epilogue

193. *Clay County News,* March 1928.
194. Duane Champlain to F.A. Sondley, May 27, 1928.
195. Newspaper clipping (date and newspaper unknown) found in the Henry Archive.

Bibliography

Abernethy, Thomas Perkins. *From Frontier to Plantation in Tennessee*. Chapel Hill: University of North Carolina Press, 1932.

Anderson, William Lee, III. *Lincoln County Men at Kings Mountain: Men Essential to the Kings Mountain Victory, 7 October 1780*. N.p.: 2009.

Annual Publication of Historical Papers. "Gov W.W. Holden and Revolutionary Documents." Series 3. Durham, NC: Historical Society of Trinity College, 1899.

Annual Report of the American Bible Society, Vol. 1. N.p.: 1838.

Arthur, John Preston. *Western North Carolina: A History (1730–1913)*. Raleigh, NC: Edward Buncombe Chapter of the Daughters of the America Revolution, 1914.

Babbage, G.F. "Notebook and Sketch Book, 1840–1850." Henry Archive (private collection).

Baer, George M. *The Natural History of Rabies*. 2nd ed. Boca Raton, FL: CRC Press, 1991.

Beatty, Francis. "Will of Francis Beatty." Will Book G, Mecklenburg County, NC.

Bedini, Silvio A. "Early American Surveyors: Mapping the Wilderness." *Professional Surveyor* (March/April 1982): 16–18, 35–36.

———. *Thinkers and Tinkers: Early American Men of Science*. New York: Charles Scribner's Sons, 1975.

Bell, Linda A. "List of Names in Christian Carpenter's Army Against the Cherokee Indians." *Footprints in Time* (1993): 106–07.

Blackmun, Ora. *A Spire in the Mountains: The Story of 176 Years of a Church and a Town Growing Together (1794–1969)*. Asheville, NC: First Presbyterian Church, 1970.

———. *Western North Carolina: Its Mountains and Its People to 1880*. Boone, NC: Consortium Press, 1980.

Blount, John Gray. *The John Gray Blount Papers*. Edited by Alice Barnwell Keith. Vol. 2. Raleigh: North Carolina Department of Archives and History, 1952.

Browder, Nathaniel C. "The Cherokee Indians and Those Who Came After: Notes for a History of Cherokee County, North Carolina, 1835–1860." Hayesville, NC, 1973.

Brown, Reverend O.L. "John Preston Arthur: Early Day Scholar, Boone Resident Historian: Plagued by Loneliness." *Watauga Democrat*, Jan 3–10, 1963.

Buchanan, John. *The Road to Guilford Courthouse: The American Revolution in the Carolinas*. New York: John Wiley and Sons, 1997.

Bunce, Oliver Bell. *The Romance of the Revolution: Being a History of the Personal Adventures, Romantic Incidents, and Exploits Incidental to the War of Independence*. New York: Bunce and Brother, 1856.

Buncombe County Register of Deeds. "Homestead Returns for W.L. Henry, 1890."

Carter, Liz. *Pioneer Houses and Homesteads of the Willamette Valley, Oregon, 1841–1865*. Portland: The Historic Preservation League of Oregon, 2013.

Colton, Henry E. *Mountain Scenery*. N.p.: W.P. Pomeroy, 1859.

Cope, Robert F., and Manly Wade Wellman. *The County of Gaston: Two Centuries of a North Carolina Region*. Gastonia, NC: Gaston County Historical Society, 1961.

Dameron, J. David. *Kings Mountain*. Cambridge, MA: Da Capo Press, 2003.

Davidson, A.T. *Reminiscences in the Lyceum*. N.p.: 1891.

Davidson, Chalmers Gaston. *Piedmont Partisan: The Life and Times of Brigadier-General William Lee Davidson*. Davidson, NC: Davidson College, 1951.

Deaver, Reuben. "Field Book of Lands Surveyed by Reuben Deaver D.S. of Buncombe County Commencing 1840." North Carolina Collection, Pack Memorial Public Library, Asheville, NC.

———. "Reuben Deaver to E.B. Dudley." Edward B. Dudley (1789–1855) Papers, 1836, North Carolina Department of Archives and History, Raleigh, NC.

Dorcas B. Henry v. Robert Henry (Haywood County, NC, 1842).

Dowd, Clement. *Life of Zebulon Vance*. Charlotte, NC: Observer Printing and Publishing House, 1897.

Draper, Lyman C. *Kings Mountain and Its Heroes: History of the Battle of Kings Mountain*. N.p.: P.G. Thompson, 1881.

Eddleman, Bill. *Abstracts of Haywood County, North Carolina, Deeds, 1808–1838*. Greenville, SC: Southern Historical Press, 2005.

Freel, Margaret Walker. *Our Heritage: The People of Cherokee County, North Carolina, 1540–1955*. Asheville, NC: Miller Printing Company, 1956.

Graham, William. "The Battle of Cowan's Ford." *The North Carolina Booklet: Great Events in North Carolina History*, July 1906: 246.

Greene, Lance. "A Struggle for Cherokee Community: Excavating Identity in Post-Removal North Carolina." PhD diss., University of North Carolina, 2009.

Gudger, Owen. "Early Historic Manuscript of Buncombe County." Unpublished, circa 1950.

Haller, Charles. "Robert Henry and His Clan." *A Lot of Old Buncombe* 28, no. 2 (May 2007): 7–15.

Hart, Albert Bushnell. *American History Told by Contemporaries*. New York: Macmillan, 1901.

Haywood, John. *A Manual of the Laws of North Carolina*. Raleigh, NC: J. Gales, 1819.

Henry, Cornelia C. *Fear in North Carolina: The Civil War Journals and Letters of the Henry Family*. Edited by Karen L. Clinard and Richard Russell. Asheville, NC: Reminiscing Books, 2008.

Henry, Dorcas B. "Last Will and Testament of Dorcas B. Henry." Buncombe County, NC, Court of Pleas and Quarter Sessions, April 1857.

Henry, James T. "Henry Family History as Dictated by William L. Henry." Whitmire, SC, 1947. Henry Archive (private collection).

Henry, Joseph. "Revolutionary War Pension Application of Joseph Henry, 1833." Revolutionary War Pension and Bounty-Land Warrant Application Files, Records of the Department of Veterans Affairs, Record Group 15, M804, National Archives, Washington, D.C.

Henry, Robert. "Account of Kings Mountain." In *Narrative of the Battle of Kings Mountain*, by David Vance.

———. "Instructions for William L. Henry." Sulphur Springs, North Carolina, May 11, 1856. North Carolina Collection, Pack Memorial Public Library, Asheville, NC.

———. "Personal Notebook of Robert Henry." Henry Archive (private collection).

Henry, Robert, and Captain David Vance. *Narrative of the Battle of Cowan's Ford, by Robert Henry; Narrative of the Battle of Kings Mountain, by Captain David Vance*. Greensboro, NC: D. Schenck, 1891.

Henry, Thomas. "Estate of Thomas Henry." North Carolina, Estate Files, 1663–1979, *FamilySearch*, https://familysearch.org/pal:/MM9.1.1/VH6X-RG5, Thomas Henry, 1791.

Henry, William L. "Unsigned Letter Relating Experiences of Thomas Henry." Henry Archive (private collection).

Holcomb, Brent H. *Deed Abstracts of Mecklenburg County, North Carolina, 1763–1779*. Greenville, SC: Southern Historical Press, 1981.

———. *Deed Abstracts of Tryon, Lincoln and Rutherford Counties, North Carolina, 1769–1786: Tryon County Wills and Estates*. Greenville, SC: Southern Historical Press, 1977.

———. *Tryon County, North Carolina, Minutes of the Court of Pleas and Quarter Sessions, 1769–1779*. Columbia, SC: South Carolina Magazine of Ancestral Research, 1994.

Howard, Mecumen Hunt. "Recollections of Tennessee." Unpublished manuscript, 1902.

Hunter, C.L. *Sketches of Western North Carolina, Historical and Biographical*. Raleigh, NC: Raleigh News Steam Job Print, 1877.

Kocin, Paul, and Louis Uccellini. *Snowstorms Along the Northeastern Coast of the United States: 1955 to 1985*. Boston: American Meteorological Society, 1990.

Kratt, Mary Norton. *Charlotte: Spirit of the New South*. Winston-Salem, NC: John F. Blair, 1992.

Laisy, Elizabeth Henry. Interviews with Richard Russell, 2008–2013.

Lanman, Charles. *Letters from the Alleghany Mountains, 1849*. North Carolina Collection, Pack Memorial Public Library, Asheville, NC.

Lincoln County, Tennessee Court of Pleas and Quarter Session, 1814-1817. W. P. A.

Logan, John H. "Robert C. Gillam to Dr. J.H. Logan, September 29, 1858." *A History of the Upper Country of South Carolina*. Charleston, SC: S.G. Courtenay and Co., 1859.

Lossing, Benson J. *The Pictorial Fieldbook of the Revolution*. New York: Harper & Bros., 1852.

Love, John. *Geodaesia; or, The Art of Measuring Land Made Easy*. London: G.G.J. and J. Robinson, 1792.

Love, Robert. "Letter: Robert Love to William Love, November 25, 1814." Love Family Records.

Low, John. *The New and Complete American Encyclopedia*. Vol. 6. New York: E. Low, 1810.

Manning, Nancy. *Buncombe County Court Records*. Vol. 1. Asheville, NC: Old Buncombe County Genealogical Society, 2009.

Marsh, Helen, and Timothy Marsh. *Early Unpublished Court Records of Lincoln County, Tennessee*. Greenville, SC: Southern Historical Press, 1993.

———. *Land Deed Genealogy of Lincoln County, Tennessee: 1828–1834*. Vol. 3. Greenville, SC: Southern Historical Press, 1996.

Mashburn, J. L. *Hominy Valley Revisited: A Journey Back to Our Favorite Times.* Enka, NC: Colonial House Publishers, 2009.

McCorkle, George. "Sketch of Colonel Francis Locke." *The North Carolina Booklet* (July 1910): 19.

McKeithen, A. "Sulphur Springs Letter: A. McKeithen to A.A. McKeithen." November 1849. Museum of the Cherokee Indian Archive, #1987.086.001, Cherokee, NC.

McLean, Dr. William. "Journey to Tennessee." *Eswau Huppeday* (Broad River Genealogical Society) 14, no. 1–3, 57–61, 95–99, 163–173.

McLean, William. "Letter, William MacLean to Mary MacLean, May 15, 1811." Raleigh, NC: North Carolina Department of Archives and History.

Medford, W. Clark. *Mountain People, Mountain Times.* Waynesville, NC: Miller Printing, 1963.

Mills, Kenneth T. "Surveying in the Mountains of Western North Carolina." In *Following in Their Footsteps: Land Surveying in North Carolina*, by Otis A. Jones. Chapel Hill, NC: Chapel Hill Press, 2006.

Moore, Mary Gudger. "Some Early Recollections of Asheville and Western North Carolina: written by Mary G. Moore at the Request of John Preston Arthur, Gaston Place." Unpublished, April 25, 1912.

Nixon, Alfred. "The History of Lincoln County." *The North Carolina Booklet* 9, no. 3 (January 1910): 111.

Olmsted, Frederick Law. *A Journey in the Back Country.* New York: Mason Brothers, 1860.

Pickens, Israel. "Letter: Israel Pickens to Robert Henry." Washington, December 16, 1812. Robert Henry Letters, #1319-z, Southern Historical Collection, The Wilson Library, University of North Carolina at Chapel Hill.

Powell, William S. *Dictionary of North Carolina Biography.* Vol. 5. Chapel Hill: The University of North Carolina Press, 1994.

Pruitt, A.B. *Abstracts of Land Entries: Buncombe Co., NC, 1794–1796.* N.p.: ABP Abstracts, 1989.

———. *Abstracts of Land Entries: Lincoln Co., NC, 1795–1797.* ABP Abstracts.

———. *Abstracts of Land Entries: Tryon and Lincoln Co., NC, 1778–1780.* N.p.: ABP Abstracts, 1987.

———. *Abstracts of Lincolnton, NC, Deeds, 1785–1868.* N.p.: ABP Abstracts, 1988.

———. *Glasgow Land Fraud Papers, 1783–1800: North Carolina Revolutionary War Bounty Land in Tennessee.* N.p.: A.B. Pruitt, 1988.

———. *Tennessee Land Entries: Military Bounty Land.* Vols. 4–6. N.p.: A.B. Pruitt, 1996.

Puett, Minnie Stowe. *The History of Gaston County*. Charlotte, NC: Laney-Smith, 1998.

Ragan, Robert Allison. *The History of Gastonia and Gaston County, North Carolina: A Vision of America at Its Best*. Charlotte, NC: Loftin & Co., 2010.

Reuben Deaver v. D.B. Henry and Robert Henry (1853).

Riggs, Brett, and Lance Greene. *The Cherokee Trail of Tears in North Carolina: An Inventory of Trail Resources in Cherokee, Clay, Graham, Macon, and Swain Counties*. Chapel Hill: University of North Carolina Research Laboratories of Archaeology, 2006.

Robert M. Henry v. W.L. Henry (1868).

Scheer, George F., and Hugh F. Rankin. *Rebels and Redcoats: The American Revolution through the Eyes of Those Who Fought and Lived It*. Cambridge, MA: De Capo Press, 1987.

Schenck, David. *Diary of David Schenck (1854–1864)*. Chapel Hill: University of North Carolina, Southern Historical Collection, 1959.

———. "Historical Literature of North Carolina: Letter to the Compiler." *Harvard University Bulletin* 7, no. 1 (October 1892): 336.

———. "Letter to the Editor, Dated September 20, 1859." *Harper's Weekly*, October 15, 1859.

Sharpe, Bill. *A New Geography of North Carolina*. Raleigh, NC: Sharpe Publishing Company, 1956.

Shepard, Dorothy. "Clay County, NC—Cemeteries—Misc. Cemeteries and Other Places of Burial." http://files.usgwarchives.net/nc/clay/cemeteries/mcopbcem.txt.

Sondley, F.A. *A History of Buncombe County, North Carolina*. N.p.: Advocate Printing Company, 1930.

———. *The Indian's Curse: A Legend of the Cherokees*. Asheville, NC: Stephens Press, 1915.

———. "Robert Henry Biography." *Asheville Citizen*, March 4, 1928.

Sondley, F.A., and T.F. Davidson. *Asheville and Buncombe County*. Asheville, NC: The Citizen Company, 1922.

Spindel, Donna. *Introductory Guide to Indian-Related Records (to 1876) in the North Carolina State Archives*. Raleigh, NC: Division of Archives and History, Department of Cultural Resources, 1979.

Strange, Robert. *Eoneguski, or, the Cherokee Chief: A Tale of Past Wars*. Washington, D.C.: Franck Taylor, 1839.

Strother, John. "Diary and Field Notes." North Carolina Collection, Pack Memorial Public Library, Asheville, NC.

Sullivan, Kathy Gunter, ed. *Civil Action Papers of Lincoln County, North Carolina, 1771–1806*. Self-published, 1989. Tennent, Gaillard S. *The Indian Path in Buncombe County*. Asheville, NC: Stephens Press, n.d.

Tennessee, State of. *Acts Passed at the First Session of the Fifteenth General Assembly of the State of Tennessee*. Murfreesboro, TN: J. Norveil, G.A. Sublett and A.C. Sublett, 1823.

Terrell, Bob. *Historic Asheville*. N.p.: WorldComm, 1997.

Tidwell, Thomas Pinckney, and Paula M. Tidwell. *Tidwell and Etherton Family*. Salt Lake City: Genealogical Society of Utah, 1991.

Vaughn, Thomas. *Space, Style and Structure: Building in Northwest America*. Vol. 1. Portland: Oregon Historical Society, 1974.

Warren, Zina. *Reminiscences of the Long Ago*. Noblesville, IN: Butler Printing House, 1911.

Wellman, Manly Wade. *Dead and Gone: Classic Crimes of North Carolina*. Chapel Hill: The University of North Carolina Press.

Wheeler, John H. *Historical Sketches of North Carolina, from 1584 to 1851*. Philadelphia: Lippincott, 1851.

Wicks, William S. *Log Cabins: How to Build and Furnish Them*. New York: Forest and Stream Publishing, 1889.

Williams, W.G. "Relating to Cherokee Nation within the Circuits of North Carolina and Its Immediate Vicinity." February 27, 1838. The King Research Collection: Trail of Tears. Manuscript copy at the Museum of the Cherokee Indian, Cherokee, NC.

W.W. Rollins and Others v. R.M. Henry and Others. 78 N.C. 342 (January 1878).

Index

A

Alexander, Rebecca/Rhoda 55
Armstrong, John 83
Articles of Agreement 96, 130

B

Baldwin. *See* preachers
Barnett, Catherine 23
Barnett's Station 79
Beal, Dick 45
Bear Creek Road 93, 97
Beattie's Ford 43
Beatty, Robert 41, 45, 58
Beatty, Thomas 22
Bee Tree Creek 52, 77
Belmont Hotel 108
Blythe, Charlotte 23
Bolin's Creek 75
Boyd, John 36
Boyles, Kate 55
Bright, James 85
Buncombe Turnpike 77
Byrd. *See* preachers

C

Campbell, William 32
Candler, C.N. 145
Candler, G.W. 102
Caney Creek 53, 90, 93, 95, 97, 114, 164
Cannon, Riley 102
Carrier, Edwin G. 108, 160
Carrier's Springs 108
Catawba River 20, 41, 49, 58, 76
  south fork 20
Cherokee
  expeditions 29, 49
  folklore 53
  land cessions 81
  land sales 125
  land surveys 91, 119
  removal (Trail of Tears) 118
  retention forts 121
Chickasaw 81, 83
Chronicle, Major William 31, 83
Coles, Alexander 83
Collins, B. 60
Compass Creek 121, 149
Corn, F.M. 107
Cornwallis, Lord Charles
  at Beattie's Ford 43

at Camden 30
at Cowan's Ford 45
leaves Charlotte 38
occupation of Charlotte 31
pursuit of Morgan 41
Cowan's Ford
battle 45, 46
description 43
General Davidson shot 45
recollections of 46
Cowpens, SC 32, 41
Crystal Creek 75
Cummings, Dr. *See* preachers

D

Davidson, A.T. 27, 71
Davidson, Colonel William 53
Davidson, General William Lee 43
Davidson, George 60
Davidson, James 55
Davidson, Mary 77
Davidson, Samuel 77
Deaver, Joseph 130
Deaver, N. 132
Deaver, Polly Henry. *See* Henry, Mary Louise "Polly"
Deaver, Reuben
death of 140
marriages 91, 129
partnership with R.M. Henry 137
postmaster 96, 125
surveys Cherokee land 118
trustee 102
Deaver, Robert P. 96, 145
Deaver, William R., Jr. 91
Dickson, Joseph 83
Dobson, Joseph 75
Dorcas B. Henry v. Robert Henry 127

E

Edmunston, Nimion 128
Elk River 81, 87, 115
Entry Taker Joe 52, 75
Erwin, Andrew 81
Erwin's Creek 75

F

Falls of Neuse Manufacturing Company 160
Ferguson, Major Patrick 31
killed 35
Fitzgerald, Samuel 130
Forked Deer River 83, 143
Fort Hembree 121
French Broad River 53, 65, 75, 77, 93, 108
Fullbright, Abraham 95, 125

G

Gamewell. *See* teachers
Gillespie, George 41
Gillespie, Robert 41
Gilmer, Enoch 33
Gilmer, William 36
Glenn, Tom. *See* preachers
Goodlake, Thomas 142
Graham, Colonel William 31
Graham, General Joseph 46
Greasy Cove 63

H

Hambright, Lieutenant Colonel Frederick 31, 34
Hawkins, James 60
Hawkins, John 102
Hawkins, William. *See* Teachers
Haywood Road 90, 97
Hendrix, Tom 108
Henry, Alexander 90, 93
Henry, Cora 145
Henry, Cornelia 107, 145, 146, 149, 158
Henry, Dorcas Bell
death 145
flees to Waynesville 118
petition for divorce 127
Henry, Edmond L. 149
Henry, Isaac 23, 67
Henry, Isabella Shields 22
Henry, James Love 117, 155, 159
Henry, Jane 22

Henry, John 24
Henry, Joseph 23
Henry, Margaret 23
Henry, Mary Louise "Polly" 91, 125, 127
Henry, Rachel 24
Henry, Robert
  as physician 67
  at Cowan's Ford 45, 46
  at Kings Mountain 33, 34, 35, 36
  at Mecklenburg Declaration of Independence 25
  bitten by fox 25
  Buncombe County solicitor 72
  clerk and master of equity 71
  clerk of the Superior Court 73
  date of birth 20
  death of 149
  defense attorney 73
  drinking 117, 118, 127, 136
  first schoolteacher 55
  in Buncombe County 55, 71
  in Cherokee Country 119
  joins South Fork Boys 31
  marriage 82
  names Compass Creek 121
  siblings 22
  surveys Cherokee land 119
  travels to Tennessee 81, 84, 115, 130
  will 158
Henry, Robert M. 96, 118, 119, 121, 136, 155
Henry, Thomas 19
  at Mecklenburg Declaration of Independence 25
  Cherokee expedition 29
  children 22
  death 22
  landowner 20
  marriage 22
  target of Loyalists 30
  with Greene 46
  with Howard and Morgan 41
Henry, William L. 30, 96, 119, 140, 160
Hominy Creek 52, 82, 90, 93, 108

I

Indian's Curse, The 53

J

Jarrett, John 82, 90, 102
Jetton, Joel 43
Jonathon's Creek 75
Jones Gap Turnpike Company 159
Jones, George W. 102
Jones, Thomas 82

K

Keener, Joseph 128
Keitt, John 100
Kings Mountain
  battle 33, 34, 35, 36
  Lincoln County militia 32
  Major Ferguson killed 35
  Major Ferguson's proclamation 31
  Overmountain Men 31
Knox, David 38

L

Leeper, James 23, 54
Leeper, Matthew 22
Lewis, Gideon 60, 62
Limestone Settlements 63
Little River Turnpike 159
Little Willow Creek 75
Locke, Colonel Francis 41
Logan, Robert 60
Long, John 84
Love, Dillard 90, 135
Love, Dorcas Bell 23
  marriage 82
Love, James 132
Love, James R. 135
Love, John 82
Love, John B. 87, 138
Love, Robert 63, 69, 82, 90, 91, 92, 130, 135
Love, Thomas 91, 131
Love, William C. 83

M

MacLean, Dr. William 76
Malvern Hills 114
Marstellar, George 149
Martin, J.G. 159
Martin, Samuel 36
Mathis, G.A. *See* teachers
Matthews, John 60
Matthews, Mussendine 57, 60, 62
Mattocks, Captain 33
McClure, John 24
McDowell, General Joseph 57, 61
McKee, James 83
McMahan. *See* preachers
Mecklenburg Declaration of Independence 26
Miller. *See* preachers
Miller, David 54
Moody, Mr. *See* preachers
Moore, Charles 102, 128, 129
Moore, Mary Gudger 88, 117
Moore, Narboone W. 129
Moore, William 52

N

Nashville Road 81
Neely, James 60, 63
Newton Academy 55
Newton, George 55
Nighten, John 42

P

Paint Creek 65
Patton, James 81
Penland, George 60
Pickens, Israel 82
Porter, Elizabeth 23
preachers
  Baldwin 103
  Byrd 103
  Cummings 103
  Glenn, Tom 103
  McMahan 103
  Miller 103
  Moody 103
  Reynolds, Reverend John 102
  Smith 103

R

Rabb, William 36
Rankin, W.D. 159
Reeves, George, Jr. 73
Reynolds, Reverend John. *See* preachers
R.M. Henry v. W.L. Henry 160
Roberts, G.M. 159
Roberts, Joshua 128, 140, 145
Robinson's Creek 75
Rollins, Pinckney 159
Rollins, W.W. 159, 160
Rutherford, General Griffith 49
Rutherford Trace 50
Rutledge, Charles 41, 43

S

Schenck, David 47
Schoenfeld, Otto B. 113
Shields, Isabella 22
Shields, Robert 22
slaves
  Alonso 155
  Andrew 135
  Andy 95, 107, 133, 135
  Athaline 155
  Ben 95
  Catherine 134
  Charles 155
  Dub 95
  Dublin 133, 135
  George 125
  Ham 125
  Hannah 90, 135
  Harriet 133, 135
  Haynes 155
  Jack 95, 119, 133
  Jim 95, 135
  John 125, 133, 134, 144

Julia 125, 133, 144
Malinda 134
Sal 135
Sam 133, 135
Sam (Buncombe Sam) 155
Sarah 125
Tena 155
Smith. *See* preachers
Smith, M. *See* teachers
Smith, Susannah 91
Smith, William D. 138
South Fork Boys 31, 34
Spencer, Joseph 68
Starret, Alexander 41
Starret, Moses 41, 43
Stines, Elias 97
Strange, Robert 69
Strother, John 57, 60
Sulphur Springs
discovery of 90
sales attempt 128, 139
Sulphur Springs Academy 102
Sulphur Springs Cemetery 100, 140, 145
Sulphur Springs Hotel
burns 107, 146
Corner House 93
descriptions of 93, 103
value of 137
Swannanoa River 52
Swannanoa Settlement 52, 77

T

Tarleton, Banastre 41
Tate, E. *See* teachers
Taylor, Mary 153
Taylor, Newton 154
teachers
Gamewell 104
Hawkins, William 102
Mathis, G.A. 102
Smith, M. 102
Tate, E. 102
Walter, T.J. 102
Terry, C.C. 108
Tidwell, Eliza Henry 129
Tidwell, Thomas P. 146, 154, 155
Tidwell, William B. 146, 153, 154
Tidwell, William G. 117, 119, 132, 144, 153
Tolliver, William 73
Tomahawk Rights 75
Torian, Mary 129
Township Tree 53
Trail of Tears 118
Tryon County Resolves 29
Tuckasegee Ford 20, 21, 42

U

Union Hill School (Academy) 55

V

Vance, David 52, 57, 60, 62, 143
Van Gilder, Thomas 160
von Ruck, Dr. Karl 108

W

Walter, T.J. *See* teachers
Warm Springs, NC 79
Waynesville, NC 69, 75, 82, 91
Weaver, John 52
Welch, L.M. 160
Wells, Mary 24
Williams, James 95
Williamson, Charles 83
Wilson, Samuel 84
W.W. Rollins and Others v. R.M. Henry and Others 160

About the Author

Richard Russell is an author who retired from the healthcare field to pursue his passion for historical research. Russell has worked on the compilations *Reminiscing with Pearl Playford: Columns from the Watervliet Record* and *My Dear Father and Mother: The Personal Letters of Livingston N. Clinard*. He has been awarded the Bob Terrell History Award by the Old Buncombe County Genealogical Society and was given special recognition by the Western North Carolina Historical Association for his work on *Fear in North Carolina: The Civil War Journals and Letters of the Henry Family*. Richard makes his home in Asheville, North Carolina.